Information Management

for voluntary & community organisations

Paul Ticher
Mike Powell

DIRECTORY OF SOCIAL CHANGE

Published by
The Directory of Social Change
24 Stephenson Way
London NW1 2DP
Tel: 020 7209 5151, fax: 020 7209 5049
e-mail: info@dsc.org.uk
from whom further copies and a full publications list are available.

The Directory of Social Change is a Registered Charity no. 800517

First published 2000

ISBN 1 900360 48 9

British Library Cataloguing in Publication Data
A catalogue record for this book is available from the British Library

Cover design by Lenn Darroux
Text design by Sarah Nicholson and Lenn Darroux
Typeset, printed and bound by Page Bros., Norwich

Directory of Social Change London Office:
Courses and Conferences tel: 020 7209 4949
Charityfair tel: 020 7209 1015
Research and Marketing tel: 020 7209 4422
Finance and Administration tel: 020 7209 0902

Directory of Social Change Northern Office:
Federation House, Hope Street, Liverpool L1 9BW
Courses and Conferences tel: 0151 708 0117
Research tel: 0151 708 0136

Contents

Acknowledgements

The authors would like to thank Anne Mountfield at the Directory of Social Change for bringing them together to collaborate on this book, and her successor Alison Baxter for all her support in its gestation.

We would also like to thank the following: London Advice Services Alliance for permission to base parts of Chapter 11 on material from Managing IT, written by Paul Ticher with Martin Jones of LASA; Oxfam for permission to base parts of Chapter 9 on Information Management for Development Organisations, written by Mike Powell.

About the authors

Mike Powell has worked on relief and development projects, first in Latin America and Africa and then in Northern England, for more than twenty years. Believing that the means form part of the end, he has always been interested in the information and communications aspects of the job. This interest has become more focused over the last ten years and he now works full time as an information management consultant for both local and international development organisations. He can be contacted on m.powell@geo2.poptel.org.uk

Paul Ticher is a consultant and trainer working with national and local voluntary organisations. He specialises in information technology and good practice in information management, including Data Protection. Much of his work experience has been in the advice and information field, including five years as IT Adviser at the Community Information Project (now absorbed into London Advice Services Alliance), where he was founder editor of Computanews. He has also worked in campaigning organisations and as Chief Officer of a small national charity. E-mail: paul@ptgt.dircon.co.uk

INTRODUCTION

The voluntary sector is awash with information. Some organisations exist to provide advice and information to clients, or need to compile information for campaigning work; for them, information is part of their core activities. Even in an organisation which concentrates on offering more direct services, handling information usually forms an important element of the work.

So why isn't the voluntary sector awash with books on how to manage information? Perhaps it is because we all handle so much information every day of our lives that we just take it for granted: 'How do I get to your house, and how long will it take?', 'What's the best medicine for this cough?', 'If my aunt is your granny's sister, how are her children related to you?'

But just as managing the office accounts is different from running a household budget, so managing information in an organisation is different from the information-handling we do in our private lives. Just because everyone already uses information all the time in their work, this doesn't mean that the information is well managed. In many organisations, in fact, rather than being badly managed, information is not really managed at all.

The norm is for people to think of an activity – next year's budget, this month's new care programme, a new project proposal – and set out to find the information they need for that activity. It is less common for people to notice that the information they produce could also help a colleague. It is still rarer for organisations to plan their use of information, to train their staff to use it well, or to link the information activities of different staff members effectively.

Different people in the same organisation can spend time looking for information that colleagues already have; much time can be spent chasing information of limited relevance; the information that is available may be so badly organised that it is not available when required. Yet there is so much information around that 'information overload' is one of the commonest complaints. Time spent looking at information as a resource which you can manage is time well spent. Information can be organised to support every other activity and to support people in doing their jobs well.

This book is intended to help you see information in a different light, as a resource which you can manage to the advantage of your organisation. There's nothing magic about it – good information management (like much of management, to be honest) is largely common sense. This book also aims to give you a few tools and ideas, and to suggest why some things usually work better than others. If it helps you apply your common sense more creatively, it will have done its job.

What is information?

In this book, information is defined very broadly, to include any data, facts, analysis, research, policy document, gossip or innuendo which is relevant to the organisation.

> 'Information is that which reduces uncertainty.' The more choice you have, the more information you need to help you make your decision.

One definition of information is that it is anything you can find out from other people. Therefore, it is different from knowledge, experience, skill or wisdom, all of which have to be learned and which are then unique to you. Two people who have access to exactly the same information may well make different decisions. This is why information management is all about making people more productive: it's what people do with information that counts. The information alone is just a resource, alongside other resources such as money, personnel, desk space, telephones, and all the other paraphernalia of a modern office.

People find information in a variety of ways: from talking to other people or reading something written long ago; happening across it or actively seeking it; piecing together different facts or data to make new information, or obtaining it ready-made. Information can come from within an organisation, generated by its own activities, and it can come from outside, from other organisations, individuals or sources. Although much of this information is in printed form, people still get a surprising amount of their information verbally, and electronic formats increasingly offer a third possibility. When considering the management of information, the information itself cannot be divorced from the activities by which it is obtained or processed.

In this book, we refer to information 'systems'. A system is one of the ways in which managers ensure that their decisions get carried out. Systems can be highly formal and prescriptive – like the procedures used to check people's benefit entitlement – or they can be informal and based on a common set of assumptions

– 'If anyone phones while I'm not here, try to get a number that I can call back on.'

In order to work well, systems don't have to be written down, but everyone has to be clear what is expected of them. In an information system, the important things to determine are usually what happens to the information and who is responsible for doing it. There may also be a need to specify the nature of the information that should be put into the system. The manager's role is to ensure that the organisation has information systems which work. If they're not working, then a little more prescription and a little less reliance on assumptions may be called for.

Good information management

Management is not an exact science. It is about analysing changing situations, taking decisions, prioritising and communicating. A manager must have good information in order to manage well, but more than that, the manager must understand that the success of the organisation also depends on how every individual member of staff uses information.

Some people mistake information management for information control, or think of a centralised, top-down system which defines who is allowed to know what, and which protects a privileged 'information elite'. These approaches don't work. There is too much information, in too many different places, for control to be possible; even if it were, restrictions on the flow of information (except for reasons of confidentiality, of course) are counter-productive.

By contrast, good information management involves supporting and enabling staff to manage information well. It involves providing staff with the necessary conditions to take individual responsibility and to apply their intelligence creatively to their task. Given the complex and fast-changing environments in which most voluntary-sector organisations work, and given their usually limited resources, maximising the effectiveness of individual staff members is essential. Good management can achieve this, monitoring the results and initiating change as necessary.

Information management can make use of formal management tools, although it does not have to. Often, it can be concerned with the mundane. Entry to the real 'information society', as opposed to that of the marketer's hype, starts with answering the phone in a helpful way and circulating the post, be it electronic or on paper, to whoever needs it.

As information is everywhere, it is not easy to write about it in a neat linear sequence. Nor is information management just a set of simple tasks which anyone can follow. It would be nice to write a book called 'Eight Easy Steps to Never Having a Problem with Information Ever Again', but managing information is not like that. At its heart, information management is about looking at the familiar – the mass of information flooding your office – in a different way and becoming able to organise and use it better. What this means precisely will vary from organisation to organisation.

'Over a third of IT executives in the UK believe information overload is responsible for their ill health, while a further 47 per cent claim it is placing a strain on their personal relationships.' *PC Pro*, March 1999, reporting on a survey commissioned by Reuters.

Knowledge management

One of the buzz-phrases of the 1990s has been 'knowledge management', much touted by heavyweight consultants and gurus. Knowledge management appears to be used in at least two different senses:

- the creation of an organisational culture in which knowledge is valued and shared, in order to maximise its benefit to the organisation.
- the use of large-scale computer technology to codify and organise knowledge which would previously have been 'locked up' inside individuals.

In both cases the underlying impetus is towards reducing the importance of the individual to the organisation and making workers far more dispensable, since they no longer have a unique value. This is tied in with 'de-layering' and 'down-sizing', whereby the company gets rid of long-standing employees who could have been relied on as the repository of a company's knowledge and experience.

The commercial logic, especially in very large organisations, is clear. For most voluntary organisations, however, knowledge management is a misleading side-track. A central theme of this book is that organisational culture should promote and support information sharing, but this should not be at the expense of valuing the additional skills, experience and knowledge that each individual brings. People are not, and should not be seen as, interchangeable.

Computer-based knowledge management systems are even more dubious. A very few successful examples (such as the development of decision-support systems for aircraft maintenance technicians) are not sufficient to show that the effort or the results are worthwhile.

About this book

This book is written for anyone concerned with management in the community and voluntary sectors, not just managers of organisations, departments or local offices but also leaders and members of small, self-managing teams or projects.

Managers know that they do not live in an ideal world. While everyone would like to be taking strategic decisions, looking forward, and developing new ways of working based on a long-term view, all too often the reality is one of coping, crisis management and trying not to get snowed under. At the same time we all know that taking decisions under pressure, without all the relevant information and without considering all the possible consequences, can create more problems for the future.

This book therefore attempts a balance. We set the overall context in which changes in the management and use of information are taking place. We also look at the most basic elements of handling information starting from how to answer the telephone or how to keep a few sheets of paper together ready for a meeting. We illustrate the issues through short case studies ('Examples') and by describing some of the information problems or 'Pressure points' common in voluntary- and community-sector organisations.

Chapter 2 describes some of the major changes taking place in the organisation, funding and working practices within the voluntary and community sectors. These changes have important implications for the sort of information organisations need and how they should handle it.

Despite the often confusing swirl of new ideas and new technologies for handling information, there are a number of distinct principles upon which effective management of information should be based. These can be applied to whatever situation you find yourself in, as a guide to a good solution. These themes are outlined in **Chapter 3** and then applied throughout the book.

Chapter 4 offers a manager's overview. It considers how the various information activities of an organisation can be looked at as a whole, as an information architecture, and how this can improve the understanding and management of information as a resource. It links this understanding to other aspects of organisational management such as strategy, personnel issues, use of technology and training.

The next three chapters – **Chapter 5,** Focusing on the information you need, **Chapter 6**, Storing information and **Chapter 7**, Sharing information internally – take a practical look at the options available for the core information-handling skills within an organisation.

Many voluntary-sector organisations are working increasingly closely with other organisations. These interactions range from joint participation in tightly contracted service delivery to voluntary participation in multi-agency partnership or sectoral advocacy and campaign groups. **Chapter 8** looks at the information flows and issues raised in managing them across organisational boundaries.

It is not a general manager's role to know everything. Knowing when and how to get help is an important part of the job. **Chapter 9** discusses some of the tools and external help available to support managers in their management of information.

Chapter 10 considers the legal issues thrown at managers by the waves of information flowing through the office. These range from the complex but at least defined, such as the impact of data-protection legislation, to the far less certain areas of on-line contracts, libel, or employees using the organisation's equipment for personal purposes.

The use of computers to support key information functions is described, when appropriate, throughout the book. **Chapter 11** follows up these references with some guidance on how the overall use of computers in the organisation can be better managed.

Finally, we look at some of the emerging trends of the 'information society'. The purpose of this book is to offer practical help for present-day problems. However, if awareness of information management is important now, it will be even more so in the future. New channels are being developed for the management and delivery of services, and for campaigning, advocacy and consultation. The pace of change is very fast and will affect every voluntary-sector organisation. **Chapter 12** identifies some important trends and suggests how voluntary-sector organisations can secure their future by looking for and taking part in new opportunities.

We also include a list of selected references and contacts for readers seeking further information about some of the subjects covered in this book. If readers are aware of other materials, or use effective techniques for information management, the authors would be interested to hear of them.

INFORMATION MANAGEMENT IN THE VOLUNTARY SECTOR

There is nothing new about information being important. What is new is the sheer quantity of information in circulation, accelerated by the increasing use of information and communications technologies in an era of huge social and economic changes. Technology enables news of change to be disseminated faster and in more detail than before, provoking more immediate responses which in turn generate further change.

The strategic implications of the nature and pace of change are considered further in Chapter 12. However, there are also major effects of change on daily work in the voluntary sector. The impact varies according to an organisation's area of activity and the extent to which it raises money directly from the public rather than through receiving grants. Nevertheless, all those working in the voluntary sector are likely to recognise most of the following trends.

Organisational changes

One result of wider social and economic changes has been the re-organisation of most large organisations, public and private, in the UK. When this started, 'being re-organised' was a major event; people tended to look forward to 'when the re-organisation is over'. It now appears that, for the foreseeable future, such re-organisation is not going to be over. Either it can be seen as a permanent process, or it can at least be expected every few years.

For smaller voluntary organisations, such re-organisation may not be internal. But every time a health service, local authority, or care service for young, elderly or mentally ill people gets reorganised, it most certainly affects the smaller organisations working in these sectors.

Changes in how work is financed

The re-organisations have tended to make public services restructure the way they contribute to the voluntary sector. The large annual core grant from a dominant public body, such as a local authority or health authority, to support a voluntary organisation's work is now rare. Organisations increasingly receive money either for project work with specified quantifiable outputs or are encouraged to bid for essentially commercial contracts. In the latter case they may be in competition with private-sector companies.

Finance from multiple sources has become a necessity for many organisations. Funders often like to see evidence that other agencies also see merit in what they are being asked to support. Thus organisations need to be aware of the strategic plans and funding priorities of a raft of European, national, regional (increasingly) and local authorities, quangos and large charitable trusts as well as the ubiquitous National Lottery. Many of these bodies are far less transparent in their decision-making and less accessible than the locally accountable public bodies which used to be the main source of funds.

Fundraising from the public has, except perhaps on a very local level, become far more competitive and requires equal attention to changing trends and new techniques.

Financing the core costs (including fundraising costs) of an organisation becomes increasingly difficult as funders want to see all their money deliver specific and directly measurable results. This restriction is of course especially onerous when it is the very changes in the funding structure which demand that the organisation puts more and more effort into identifying partners, presentation, liaison and reporting.

Demands for more professionalism

Many of the new funding arrangements operate in a commercial culture. Instruments of commercial practice such as business plans, quantifiable outputs and 'glossy' presentations are expected as a matter of course. Such instruments are often useful planning and management tools – although they can be expensive to develop and use. Many issues of process – for example, concepts like empowerment – do not, however, lend themselves to measurement in the same language as monthly sales figures. They may also cause problems by creating different 'languages' for the project's funders on the one hand and its beneficiaries on the other. This can be difficult for the voluntary organisation in the middle to manage, creating divergent expectations and problems of project ownership.

Almost all voluntary organisations are affected by the vast increase in the amount of reporting and monitoring demanded by funders. Where once funding bodies may have been prepared to act on a general sense of an organisation being 'a good thing', or on anecdotal evidence of its work, now the emphasis is very much on producing hard statistics which can be verified and audited. Assessing quality of service can be a valuable exercise. However, staff may feel under pressure if each funder insists on its own set of measures, regardless of how compatible these are with each other or with how the voluntary organisation itself would prefer to assess its performance.

The information management issue here is how to carry out a worthwhile amount of monitoring for the organisation's own purposes, and produce the reports required by funders without over-burdening the staff in paperwork.

These new requirements may or may not improve an organisation's performance, but they do put it under immediate pressure. In the old days it might have been possible to write an annual report by delving into project files to come up with a selection of results that would satisfy all the readers in one go. But if you are required to provide quarterly reports in different formats to a number of different funders, you have to plan from the start how you are going to satisfy them all.

Pressure for partnership

Another relatively recent trend has been the expectation for organisations to work in partnerships that include both community and voluntary organisations and those from the public and private sectors. When such partnerships are genuine, their existence greatly broadens the scope of what may be achieved. Others are clearly little more than marriages of convenience arranged by dominant local bodies in order to meet the criteria of their funders.

Faced with a partnership opportunity, a manager first needs information about the prospective partners, and their reasons for wanting the link, as a basis for negotiation. If the joint project goes ahead it throws up considerable additional information management issues, including 'ownership' of information, mechanisms for sharing it and storing it, confidentiality, and responsibility for quality of data.

New technologies

While dealing with the types of change outlined above, workers and organisations also have to grapple with adopting new technologies. In a confused and permanently changing marketplace, they seldom have the time to learn about these in sufficient detail or to use them to their full potential. Stories of computer disasters in the voluntary sector (as anywhere else) could fill a book, although whether it would be shelved under comedy or tragedy is open to debate. Despite these experiences, substantial parts of the voluntary sector have been quick to adopt new technologies. The question for most now is not whether to use these technologies, but how to use them best to serve organisational objectives.

For there are disadvantages as well as advantages. Photocopiers, computers, fax machines, mobile phones and the Internet mean that more information reaches people, in more different ways, than ever before. For individuals, this leads to information overload; for organisations it is a management headache. Where once it may have been true that the aim was to maximise the amount of information available, now it is more a case of filtering it down to the essentials. The key question is how to achieve this reduction to manageable quantities of information without completely cutting off your access to the external information which you need.

> 'Unlimited electronic information, if unmanaged, will "drown" employees. "If you take human interaction away you can reduce people's effectiveness and enjoyment. After all, it's for the interaction with other people that we come to work.".' Review of *Nil by Mouth*, from Investors in People UK and Arthur Andersen, in *People Management*, 15 October 1998.

The consequences of change

All these organisational changes, which are mainly externally driven, inevitably have a strong effect on the sector. Voluntary agencies that are unable to organise themselves to work in the prescribed ways can find it harder to operate or to attract the necessary funding. Voluntary-sector organisations need to be able to respond quickly to new opportunities and threats and they need to be highly flexible in how they do so. This inevitably involves greater staffing flexibility – including the use of short-contract, sub-contract or part-time staff members, which in turn raises new management and information challenges.

All these changes demand increasing attention to information and communication in your organisation. As a manager, you must do the following.

- Ensure that staff members and volunteers each know what their information role is and are able to perform it.
- Collect enough information about your organisation's activities, clients, members, contacts, staff and volunteers to assess the value of its work and enable it to plan ahead.
- Ensure that technology for handling the information that flows into, within and out from your organisation is used effectively and responsibly.
- Be alert to re-organisations or policy reviews of the large agencies active in your sector, in order to understand the possible implications.
- Constantly review potential sources of financial support and any changes of policy or direction among them.
- Be aware of the potential benefits and dangers of partnerships with other organisations.

- Meet the various planning, accounting, reporting and evaluation needs of your different funders and of the different partnerships in which you are involved.
- Do all of the above without losing the trust of your core constituency or beneficiaries, nor the ability to deliver work of real meaning to them.

It is because it is not easy to perform such a range of information activities that information has to be consciously managed!

ESSENTIAL PRINCIPLES

Although this book contains numerous practical suggestions, we would not like these to be seen as fixed and immutable. All our suggestions are based on fundamental principles, and it is more important to understand these than it is to follow lists of what to do. Some of the principles reinforce this point by their nature. We argue, for example, that information management should be 'people-oriented', meaning oriented to the people you work with. Your people may be different – in terms of gender, culture or age, working hours and arrangements, or motivation – from ours or anyone else's. The most perfect system designed for our people may be of no interest to yours, but the principle applies to all.

This links with another of our principles which is that an information system and its management have to be dynamic. Some organisations, especially large bureaucracies, see systems as massive and unchanging. How often have you been infuriated by being told – often as a customer, sometimes as a citizen – that you cannot have something which is yours by right because 'the system' or 'the computer' can't do something in a certain way. Until very recently indeed, textbooks for systems analysts and computer programmers were telling their students in effect that 'your job is to write a system which meets the organisation's information needs. These do not change.' This is rubbish. They change all the time. It is quite possible that some of the practical tips we offer will be inappropriate to you now, very useful next year and redundant the year after. The permanent advice is in the principles.

These principles can be grouped under four main headings. Information management needs to be:

- people-oriented
- defined
- dynamic and
- realistic

The rest of this chapter presents a brief explanation of each of these groups of principles.

Make information systems people-oriented

The most important quality measure for any way of organising information is whether the people using it find it helpful as they try to do their job. This means people as they are, not how an ideal system would find it more convenient for them to be. People develop short-cuts, make intuitive connections, and screen out large amounts of the information potentially available to them, often without realising it. Any system that works with the grain of human nature is far more likely to be productive.

Managing information therefore needs to be based on an understanding of what staff or other users would like, what is easiest for them, what is the most intuitive. Part of this understanding is likely to be that different people have different needs and different ways of doing things. The more these differences can be accommodated within a framework which also supports the organisation's needs, the better everything is likely to work.

Another vital element is to show people that you value and use the information which they produce. If the organisation does not need such information, it should not be asking people to produce it. A people-oriented approach should also encourage people to take responsibility for the information they use and produce. This means making the information component of any jobs clear to those doing them. It means thinking of information requirements in the selection and development of staff. It means rewarding good practice. It also means being clear what the minimum requirements of any system are and what sanctions will be taken against people who do not comply with them.

Another aspect of being people-oriented is that you cannot plan systems for other people in the abstract. You should always consult potential users about any system you are developing and encourage feedback once it is in operation.

Define your information resources

For information to be used effectively, it is necessary to be able to answer the following questions.

- Where is the information, and in what format? Is it electronic, printed, hand-written, in people's heads?
- What is it? Is it part of the accounts? Is it collected for monitoring project activities? Is it used for programme planning? Is it in your client files or membership records?
- How accurate does it need to be? For example, it is usually necessary for accounting information to be more accurate than the address list for a free-subscription newsletter. Time and money should be spent on ensuring that information is of adequate quality for its purpose. It doesn't make sense to spend more than that.

■ What are its source and status? Did you produce the information yourselves? If not, do you know where it came from and how reliable the source is?

Defining your information resources in this way is the starting point for spotting how information collected for one purpose can in fact – possibly in conjunction with some other information or with some change in format – be used for another. Wherever possible, the aim should be to collect information once and then use it and re-use it for a multitude of purposes. For instance, with careful planning, some basic figures on cost or income collected at a point of service delivery can be used for: accounts, monitoring the preferences of beneficiaries, reporting to funders and planning new work.

Take a dynamic approach

Any organisation in which the information flows are not changing all the time is one which is not responsive enough to the world around it. There are two aspects to this. Firstly, it is not enough to ensure that a neat internal 'information system' is working as planned. The voluntary sector survives on its ability to have an impact on the world in which its beneficiaries live. That world and the arrangements available for the development and care of its people and environment are changing constantly. Any voluntary-sector organisation there-fore needs to be outward-looking and alert for change. The priorities it sets for its information management need to reflect such an attitude.

Secondly, information itself benefits from 'movement': it acquires value when it is exchanged. Much information becomes significant only when it is compared with some from another place or time, or is linked with other information to form a larger picture.

Be realistic

No matter how much we stress the importance of information management, it is vital to remember that its purpose is to support the work of the organisation. This purpose is defeated if you or anyone else in the team gives so much attention to perfecting the information systems that other important work is not done. The importance of not overdoing it is reinforced by the need for any information system to be dynamic and capable of rapid change.

You should also remember that what actually happens is more important than what is supposed to happen. If news is spread within half an hour by rumour, a memo that goes round in a few hours time isn't fulfilling the requirements. Whenever you are reviewing your information system make sure that you find out what is really going on, not just what 'the system' says should happen.

Nor should information management be exempt from the requirement that resources applied to it should generate some positive return. How to measure this, with a resource as complex as information, is not always easy. However, the principle remains that a manager should know what benefits are expected from an investment in information management, and should have some way of checking whether the benefits have been created.

Finally, although we have stressed that everyone – and particularly every manager – should take responsibility for information, this is not to belittle relevant specialist skills such as classification, filing, archiving, librarianship and expertise in information and communications technologies. One point of having a better understanding of the issues involved is to know when to use specialist help and how to get the most value out of it.

INFORMATION AND THE ORGANISATION: THE MANAGER'S OVERVIEW

Since information needs managing just like any other resource, the manager's tasks include:

- understanding the role of information in the organisation's overall strategy.

- drawing up a specific information strategy if appropriate, but in any case setting priorities for information activities.

- ensuring that staff job descriptions and roles support good information management.

- encouraging a climate of good information practice and ensuring that this is managed well, right down the line.

- being able to analyse the use of information within the organisation and identify problem areas.

- establishing procedures and policies for information handling and management, including confidentiality and Data Protection.

- ensuring that information technology is well managed.

- ensuring that staff have the resources they need to get on with the job, including information-handling and IT skills.

The manager should also set a good example by managing their own information well. All these areas are discussed in the remainder of this book.

The list may appear daunting. It is worth remembering that many aspects of good information management actually make life easier, or can be incorporated into other things that you would be doing anyway. However, it is easy to underestimate the amount of time and/or money involved in setting up and running more formal information systems, whether paper-based or on computer. The manager's priority should normally be to get existing activities working better before embarking on ambitious new initiatives with impossible goals.

An information strategy

Priorities should be based on a strategy, even if it is not expressed in any detail. A strategy should be an overall framework for an organisation or for a strand of its activity. Its aim should be to give clear guidance about what the organisation is trying to achieve and how. Thus, for example, a housing charity may believe that its best chance of being able to provide the services it wants to is by winning new local authority contracts and reducing its dependence on trust income and donations. If such a strategic change is accepted and communicated then it provides a clear framework within which staff can operate. They will be aware that attending a conference on managing contracts will be a better use of their time than researching affinity fundraising.

A strategy is not the same as a plan. A strategy should provide the overview within which more detailed plans can be made with the confidence that they are in line with what the organisation is trying to achieve.

Rather than talk of an information strategy in isolation, we would argue that it is more important for organisations to give serious and explicit attention to information within an overall strategy. This needs to be on two levels:

- the role of information in what the organisation is trying to achieve; and
- the role of information management in how it should be achieved.

Practical exercise

The next time you are faced with making a decision that is clearly information-related, make a point of writing down the strategic priorities on which you are basing your decision. Whenever you need to make a similar decision thereafter, go back to your notes and see if anything has changed in your priorities before thinking about the new proposals.

There are many examples of information itself having a strategic role. For instance, it has long been recognised that giving charitable handouts alone will not reduce poverty. Many charities now work towards their aims by marshalling information to support a campaign for political change alongside their direct services. New means of collating and presenting information have led many more organisations to increase the priority they give to information activities as a core part of their work.

Giving information such priority emphasises the need to manage it well. An organisation which is already doing this may not need a separate information strategy in order to meet new strategic goals. It may be possible simply to draw up some new plans in order to ensure that the strategy is properly supported. However, in other cases more thought and attention needs to be given to how an organisation is actually going to achieve its new goals.

Another context in which 'information strategies' are often discussed is that of information technology. It is not unusual for changes in technology to be one of the catalysts that prompt an organisation into thinking about its approach to information management in general.

Example 1 Time for a new strategy

Mark is the campaigns officer of a small environmental pressure group. Over the years, the group has built up a reputation for the quality of its information in its specialised area. Until now the main route for disseminating the information has been by post to paying subscribers. Every month, Mark produces a detailed bulletin which is sent out to a mailing list of around a thousand people. The income from this service has been one of the main ways in which the group funds its work.

Recently, however, the number of people using the service has been tailing off. When Mark investigates, he finds that the main reason is that people can now find much of the same information on the Internet. Although this may well cost them as much (in phone and other charges) as it previously did to subscribe to Mark's service, they prefer it because it gives them access to a wider range of information sources, many of which are more up to date than a paper service could ever be.

This poses a dilemma for Mark's organisation. Simply creating a Web site for the organisation would not provide it with the income previously generated by the current service. Instead, Mark and his colleagues decide that they need to look again at why they collect information, who they collect it for, how they distribute it and how the whole process is funded.

Eventually they decide to carry on with their specialist information work, and to distribute it, not through their own Web site, but through an established site set up by a similar organisation. To replace the lost income, however, they decide to develop expertise in carrying out environmental audits, instead of charging for their factual information.

Information economics

You might have ambitions to develop the most all-encompassing information system ever dreamed of, just as you might like to move your organisation's offices to the penthouse suite of the best office block in town. The chances are that you can afford to do neither. You will have to make choices between spending money or time on one information activity rather than another, or between an information activity and something completely different. 'Information activity' in this context covers a multitude of possibilities, from expanding your library or buying a personal computer to having a working lunch with a colleague from another organisation.

To make those choices it is necessary to have some basis for judging the likely benefit which any expenditure will produce. Some information choices have a direct cost-benefit effect – for example, if you need to send the announcement of a meeting to 20 people, it is much cheaper to e-mail it than to photocopy and post it.

Example 2 Economy through e-mail

Jasvinder is convenor of a group of advice centres that negotiate jointly for local-authority support. At a time of cuts, the weeks before the council budget decisions were always full of draft proposals, counter proposals and panic in all its forms. All significant information had to be photocopied and posted to the 35 member organisations. Each mailing cost £35 in postage and copying plus several hours of Jasvinder's time.

When e-mail was first considered as an option, it did not make economic sense. Not all the advice centres had computers let alone modems; very few had e-mail addresses; and some of the documents involved were not available on disk.

Over time, all the centres have acquired computers and most now have e-mail. All documents are now written on compatible word-processors. Jasvinder realises that the cost of upgrading the federation's equipment and skills will easily be recouped by savings from its use of e-mail instead of the post to the majority of its members. The economics of deciding to upgrade – at the right time – were easy.

However, many other activities cannot be so easily assessed. How do you know whether the factor that scuppered your funding bid was a lack of well-researched, good-quality information, especially if the trust you applied to was one of those which do not give feedback? How do you value, working in a not-for-profit context, that extra piece of knowledge which enables you to add happiness to a service that you are providing for children? The answer is that you cannot. What you can do is to understand the ways in which information may create value – be it in monetary or in some other form.

The many ways in which information activities can create value for your organisation include:

- direct return on investment, such as in Example 2;
- improved quality of service to your beneficiaries through being better informed of their needs or up to date with new developments in the field;
- the provision of information as a service for your beneficiaries;
- improved internal management leading to better use of resources or the increased satisfaction of funders;
- the production of better and better-argued plans or projects, leading to more support, future work and positive outcomes;
- improved knowledge of the external environment so that you get earlier warning of threats and opportunities;
- a better image.

It is often hard to measure the potential value quantitatively.

Example 3 Which information development?

Joyce is the manager of a small charity working with older people. She receives two proposals, each requiring money from her small 'information development' budget.

1 To develop a Web page for the charity. This, it is argued, will raise the charity's profile in the local community, explaining the services the charity offers. It will also be part of a local 'partnership network' and thus illustrate the charity's commitment to working in partnership with others.

2 To conduct a survey of older people living locally who do not participate in the charity's activities, in the hope that this will increase understanding of older people's needs and of how the charity can improve its services or change its image to serve more people.

There is no direct comparison possible between the two proposals. Joyce decides to support the second proposal because she believes it may lead to the improvement of services, may provide evidence to support funding applications for the charity's work and is a one-off proposal. She believes that the Web page would not at present be the best way of

---

publicising services to the charity's target group (older people). She is also aware that good Web pages require constant updating, and so is concerned about the costs of maintaining the site after its initial design and production is complete. She is committed to local partnerships but believes that these should be based on the realities and priorities of their members.

What Joyce is doing here is making a series of subjective judgements about the value of each proposal to her organisation and its clients. Although subjective, such judgements do not have to be haphazard or casual. Even though it is often not possible to quantify the value produced by information – especially in advance, when the decision is being made – the process should still be consistent.

The reasons behind decisions should always be recorded so that in future the decisions can be analysed to monitor whether they have led to the desired outcomes. They can also be standardised so that the questions asked of each proposal are the same. Such questions should be related to the organisation's goals. For example:

- How would the information produced by this proposal contribute to meeting our overall strategic aims?
- Would it help us meet or monitor any immediate targets we have set ourselves?
- How would it contribute to meeting the aims of our information strategy?
- Will it contribute positively to our use of information technology?

Analysing your information patterns

The basic building blocks of any strategy are to know: where you are; where you want to be; and, in general terms, how you are going to get there. In the context of information this requires starting with a clear understanding of how you are currently managing your information.

This means knowing or finding out:

- what information you use;
- where it comes from;
- who does what to it;
- where it goes;
- where it is stored, and in what format;
- who is responsible for it;
- what quality is maintained.

These questions may be asked in different ways in different organisations. For example, a large organisation might ask them at the level of departments while a small one might work at the level of individuals. The process of asking them may be more or less formal. The purpose however is the same – by asking simple questions, to tease out answers to more fundamental questions.

- Is it easy to get a picture of what happens to information in the organisation?
- Do people know who is responsible for what? Who uses what they produce? Where they can find what they want?
- Is there evidence of duplication? Has the exercise shown areas where information collected for one purpose could be used for another?
- Does all the information activity identified serve a useful purpose?
- Does the organisation have information needs which are not currently being met?

The process of asking these questions and reflecting on the answers is sometimes called an **information audit**. The word audit is most often associated with accounting, when it often means an occasional event involving the presence of outsiders. We prefer to think of an information audit as the starting point of shaping an **information architecture** for an organisation – the framework of goals, policies, procedures and behaviour within which the staff carry out their information activities.

How to use an information audit

Whatever it is called – audit, evaluation, or review – the process of asking questions should give a good picture of what is happening with information in an organisation. The output is often a diagram or map which shows how information does or does not flow round the organisation, although, for those who dislike graphical presentations, there is no reason why the process cannot be written out. The formality and detail of the output can vary from beautifully formulated computer graphics to sketches on the backs of envelopes. What is important is that the information is recorded and then used. It can be used in a number of ways.

- The picture generated can be used to reflect on some of the five fundamental questions listed above. Does the current picture show satisfactory use and management of information? If it does not, what can be improved?
- The existing picture can help people to imagine a better one, and the existence of a 'current' information picture alongside a 'future' one can greatly aid the planning of changes in information management desired as a result.
- It is an opportunity to involve people in the whole process. It can be used just by senior managers and consultants, but may be more beneficial if as many people as possible are involved. Such involvement – defining information

needs and learning the needs of those you supply with information – can be highly motivating. Information is of interest to everyone: the office cleaners need to know which meeting rooms will be free in order to plan their work effectively, just as the finance director needs information on next year's budget.

- The analysis can also be used as a tool for monitoring. The picture of what should be happening can be communicated in such a way that everyone knows what is supposed to happen in their area of work – what information comes from and goes to where. You can then find out if information is flowing as planned and if it is meeting people's needs.

- It is a tool for planning new activities. An organisation may come across an opportunity to carry out a new project or some new line of activity. Traditionally this will lead management to consider implications for staffing, office-space and finances. The existence of an information architecture will bring an understanding of information issues – which will in turn illustrate staffing and financial issues – to the process of decision-making.

- Finally it can contribute clear insights into the way information is used when the development of information technology within the organisation is being discussed.

Daily management interventions

Even if your situation does not warrant a full-scale information audit, as a manager you need to be aware of what is going on, and continually asking the right questions.

- Devise methods for tracking what is being spent directly on information and in terms of staff time and computer expenditure. If you have not done this before you should probably be sitting down when you look at the figures - but don't panic, it may all be money well spent.

- Regularly ask staff in supervision sessions what use they are making of the information they receive or produce, and whether it is the most useful type or in the best form for them – this can be part of a review of the information architecture.

- Periodically survey staff members to find out how much they are using information from expensive bought-in sources – conferences, subscriptions, books. (A lack of use does not automatically mean that the source is of no value to you but it does raise questions.)

- Require project proposals, designs for lobbying campaigns and other important documents used for internal decision-making to list the sources of information for what is proposed. This both indicates what has been found valuable and can be used to evaluate the proposal in question – are the sources good, do they show variety, and whose voice is being heard?

- Ask external contacts what they think of information provided by your organisation. Is it useful? Is it convincing? Does it mark out your organisation as being more thoughtful or professional or better informed than others?

Computers and information management

Although computers are a significant component of information technology, that does not necessarily mean that they are the appropriate technology for all information-handling tasks. They are certainly not a cure for every ill, and you won't solve your problems by throwing a computer at chaos - you'll just end up with computerised chaos. Computers are also expensive: if your database is unproductive or your Web site is not visited, you will have wasted considerable amounts of money, time and effort.

Fundamentally, computers are just tools, albeit very complex ones. It is the skill with which they are used, not the technology itself, that determines the outcome. If you try to make a cake just by guessing at the ingredients, it doesn't matter how swish your oven and baking equipment, there is absolutely no guarantee that the result will be edible. Even if you follow a recipe, the more experience you have, the better the outcome is likely to be.

Correspondingly, if an amateur has a go at developing a database or a Web site, the result is unlikely to work well and could be disastrous, even if they are using 'professional' tools. If you are serious about your information-handling, you will only undertake projects that you know can be competently carried out.

The complexity of computers can be a draw-back in itself. Most tasks on a computer have a certain minimum start-up time. Who would bother turning on their computer and waiting for it to power up, then loading their word-processor just to take down a telephone message? They can also impose limitations; few database systems offer the flexibility of a card index for adding unstructured notes, for example, or you find that the system won't let you enter people's names in the format they prefer.

In the end it comes down to being clear about your goals, then taking a hard-headed decision. So you have to work out what you want to do, and sort out your processes and systems first, then see where and how the computer can help. This might well mean taking professional advice.

Despite the limitations outlined above, computers do play an important role in information management. They may even allow you to offer new services or do things that could not be undertaken with traditional methods. Key uses include:

- databases to hold quantities of structured information about people, organisations, services or issues;
- word-processing to produce printed documents;

- spreadsheets for automating calculations and presenting figures;
- e-mail as a means of communication:
- the Internet as a source of information;
- the Web as a publishing medium;
- on-line trading as a way of selling products or services.
- specialised programs for handling accounts or statistics.

These applications are discussed in more detail at relevant places in following chapters.

The people side of information work

Even the best decisions need to be carried out in order to have an effect. Getting the staff to implement decisions, especially where these involve changes to long-established and comfortable ways of working, is therefore one of the main challenges a manager faces. You may, for example, need to ensure that people:

- understand the importance of information in their work and for the organisation.
- take responsibility for collecting information in a reliable and usable format.
- become better at sharing relevant information at the right time, and in the most appropriate way.
- learn how to cope with information overload.
- give accurate and appropriate information to clients, enquirers and the like.
- respect confidentiality and do not share information beyond appropriate boundaries.

Getting people to think about their own and others' information needs, and getting them to trust other people as sources of expertise, may mean a change in their way of working or in your organisation's culture. Such changes are not always easy to bring about.

As with any management issue, the key points are:

- be very clear about what sort of behaviour you value;
- offer people appropriate training if they need it;
- find a suitable way to notice and reward 'good' behaviour (this requires some form of monitoring);
- if necessary, impose penalties on people who don't comply.

Above all, you have to mean it. The direction of change should be non-negotiable, although the means of getting there could well be the subject of discussion and modification.

If things don't appear to be working, or moving in the direction that you want, forcing them through may not be the best solution. Always ask yourself and your staff why people aren't doing what you want. There may be a genuine reason why your solution doesn't work, or factors that you didn't take sufficiently into account.

Example 4 Implementing a non-negotiable policy

Your organisation has decided to centralise its diary, so that the person answering the phone knows what to tell callers when people aren't available. Inevitably some of the staff are going to be more conscientious than others about filling in the diary. What should you do?

- This has to be non-negotiable. The system will only work if everyone complies.
- Make clear what you expect, in whatever way is most appropriate. A meeting gives people the chance to ask questions and raise issues. You may need to back up your decision in writing, so that no one has the excuse that they didn't know what was expected.
- Answer questions such as: 'How long do I have to be out of the office or in a meeting before it has to be in the diary?' 'What is the procedure if I am called away in an emergency or kept out longer than expected?' There are bound to be issues like this. Try to lay down general principles, rather than masses of detailed directions.
- Training is unlikely to be an issue in this example, but you may want to have a formal trial period of, say, a week, when everyone involved is expected to record problems and think how they might have been resolved.
- Once the system is in place there are at least two possible ways of monitoring it. You could do spot checks: look in the diary, see where people are supposed to be, and check if they really are. Or the person in charge of the diary could be asked to record times when they used the system but the person they wanted wasn't where they said they would be.
- Use this information to offer rewards or draw problems to people's attention.

Does this sound more heavy-handed than you are used to? Perhaps it does, but that's what non-negotiable means.

The changes in behaviour you are likely to want will range from the specific, as in Example 4, to the far more general. The most important of these is the move from hoarding information as a potential source of individual power and prestige to sharing information as a potential source of value for the organisation. Such a change does not come automatically. Nor is it as easy to measure as something like checking the entries in a diary. However, it is worth giving your attention first to directing and then to monitoring what is happening. If the organisation carries on rewarding people indiscriminately, whether they selfishly concentrate on their own tasks or take the trouble to share information of value to others, then the desired change will not happen at all.

Example 5 Incentive to e-mail

Naomi, the Chief Officer of a large organisation wanted to encourage her senior managers to learn how to use computers better, particularly for e-mail, so she introduced a new policy that expenses claims would be met only if they were submitted electronically – not because it suited the accounts department particularly, but because once people had learned to use the equipment for something they needed badly, they would be more likely to see its potential in other situations as well.

Example 6 Reviewing a system that isn't working

When Brian took over as Information Officer in a national organisation, he couldn't work out why staff weren't putting information into the new database consistently, despite all his instructions. Eventually he realised that the people who were expected to put the information in had not been consulted when the database was designed, so they couldn't get information out in a format that was any use to them. All the output was geared to the needs of managers. Once the system had been redesigned so that everyone could see practical benefits of using it, the quality and comprehensiveness of the data improved dramatically.

Practices from personnel management

Many practices standard in personnel management can be adapted to emphasise the importance an organisation is giving to how staff handle information.

- A job description should be clear – in general terms – about what information is likely to be handled by the person doing the job and who they should be receiving information from and passing information to.
- A person specification should stress the type of information-handling skills and attitudes required along with consideration of how these are going to be assessed during the selection process.

- Appraisal and supervision should include assessment by other colleagues, not just by more senior managers, of an individual's information practice. Remember, the people who most benefit from someone's openness with information are not necessarily their managers but their colleagues, or even their counterparts in partner organisations.
- Use external sources of monitoring as well. When one advice centre asked its clients about the quality of the service they received, one of the workers was shown to be consistently bad at explaining things. The centre was able to use this feedback to help the worker identify ways to improve.

Example 7 Information responsibilities in a job description

All roles have information responsibilities, not just the obvious ones. A development worker, for example, may have to:

- Record information about activities undertaken concisely, systematically, in good time, in the manner set out by The Agency.
- Participate in the central diary and contribute to the central contact database of organisations The Agency works with.
- Ensure that colleagues are made aware of developments which may affect their area of work.
- Respect the confidentiality of clients and abide by The Agency's confidentiality policy.

Technology-led monitoring

In all the discussion of monitoring, it is important not to go overboard. Although software can be used to measure how many keystrokes an hour someone is entering on their keyboard, while swipe cards can automate clocking on, such intrusive monitoring does nothing for staff morale and is generally of questionable value to managers, particularly in the voluntary sector.

Monitoring may be appropriate in some cases, such as:

- e-mail records and Web access logs, in order to ensure that the organisation's Acceptable Use Policy is being followed.
- random monitoring of telephone enquiry services for quality control purposes.
- monitoring staff in vulnerable situations for security purposes.

Where monitoring is carried out, it is important that staff and, if applicable, others know that it is being done, and that appropriate safeguards are in place.

Training other staff and managers

Through a decision to offer training, and through the subjects of the training offered, an organisation can send clear messages about its priorities. Even if you are not making dramatic changes, training in information management may well pay dividends. However, if you are introducing new systems or practices you should certainly expect to train staff and their managers, and should plan this in from the beginning.

Some changes may be perceived as very difficult. Even a simple change of word processing package may cause resentment and concern if it is not handled properly. The key is to support staff through their understandable worries, while making it clear that the organisation's needs are the ultimate priority.

Since information style is often seen as very much a personal preference or individual habit, new ways of working may be seen as an infringement of personal choice. There is nothing wrong with insisting on the legitimate needs of the organisation, provided part of the strategy also encourages people to take individual responsibility and initiative. Internal courses or coaching pro-grammes, where staff can have the reasoning behind the changes explained, may be more appropriate than external ones.

Beware also of using external training courses to mask internal conflicts or tensions. Where there is a genuine difficulty or disagreement, it is much better to tackle it more directly, rather than sending people on courses – even courses in conflict management.

Training on information and its management can take a number of forms.

Training workshops. Information management lends itself well to collaborative approaches to training. Workshops involving people who depend on each other for information will almost invariably raise their awareness of information issues and identify areas for improvement. These can either be tackled there and then, feed into the planning of an information architecture, or define needs for more formal training.

Revision of existing training practice. Some training takes place too much in isolation. Of course a training session needs to be focused on whatever outcome is desired, but the wider context for all activities involves information. All training should seek to relate the particular topic to relevant information issues.

Training in information management. Virtually all the techniques and tools described in this book can be acquired or developed through training, although suitable courses are thin on the ground. This might include training:

■ to improve people's personal information-handling skills;

- in the general use of computers – often essential if expensive machines and software are to be used efficiently;
- in time management, which often has an information-handling element – but needs to be carefully assessed for quality;
- in the specific practices of an organisation – how to use our filing system or our database, for example – so that one person doesn't accidentally undermine the collective value of what everyone else has done;
- in how to apply general skills in a specific context – a trained researcher may not be aware of the detailed sources available on the Internet in the very specific area he or she has been hired to cover, for example. (This type of training may also be provided through one-to-one **coaching**, rather than through a formal course.)

Mutual support or non-managerial supervision. Since changes in information-handling practice often take time, this area is particularly suitable for regular short periods of contact with either an internal or external 'buddy' or mentor.

'"They didn't give me any training in how to manage the information or what was important", [Di Harris] says. "I had to work 13 or 14 hours a day coping with thick wodges of computer printouts, e-mails, 30 to 40 memos a day and notes. No one had time to listen." ... Saul Wurman, the US guru, who coined the phrase "information anxiety", says it is produced by the "ever widening gap between what we understand and what we think we should understand. Information anxiety is the black hole between data and knowledge."' From an article by Victor Keegan in The *Guardian*, 5 November 1996.

chapter ⑤

FOCUSING ON THE INFORMATION YOU NEED

Information in an organisation is like steam in an engine. Applied in the right place, it is enormously powerful. However, in order to do this work it has to be directed to the right place. Left with nowhere to go it can build up until the pressure is too great, with catastrophic results.

Everyone is familiar with the overflowing in-tray or the pile of unread magazines. Then there are the interruptions, from phone calls, colleagues, faxes and e-mails, and the worry that if they are not attended to, some vital piece of information will go unnoticed. All of this stops people from getting on with what they should be doing, and makes them feel frustrated.

One of the keys to managing information well, therefore, is to be selective. One aspect of this is to cut out as much as possible that is not needed. If we can do this, both for ourselves and, as managers, for our organisations, we have created some free space in which to be more creative about how we handle the remaining information.

> 'The average manager sends or receives up to 178 messages per day, with many messages being duplicated in both paper and electronic form.... The phone is still the most popular form of communication, accounting for 56 of the daily messages.' *PC Pro*, September 1997, reporting on research commissioned by Pitney Bowes.

It is important to ensure that the information we do have is used and re-used as often as possible, instead of 'new' information being created each time we need it. This applies particularly when we look at statistics and information that is used for monitoring an organisation's activities. Good management often depends on having the right information, but often it seems too difficult or time-consuming to obtain it. In fact, the information may be there, but just not in the right form, and a little effort in redesigning the way it is recorded or stored may be all that is needed to make it more available. That is why it is always worth looking at this area first – it feels good, it makes a difference, and it reduces the amount of additional work rather than creating more.

Pressure point

I don't know what to do with all the information that comes into our organisation.

Information pours into most organisations. Just some of the sources include: magazines, newsletters and regular mailings, specific research that generates reports, phone calls, Internet searches, answers to letters, gossip, minutes of meetings, publicity material from other organisations, and in the heads of the staff.

You should:

- be clear what sort of information your organisation needs, and emphasise what is most important.
- reduce the flow of less important material (but not to the extent of withdrawing your antennae completely from the outside world);
- allocate the work of sifting material to people who know what they are looking for;
- ensure that each piece of information is handled as few times as possible;
- have 'a place for everything and everything in its place'.

Example 8 Using the information to hand

Wilma is the Membership Secretary of a small charity. The Committee wants to know whether people tend to join and renew their membership at particular times of the year, in response to the organisation's activities, but Wilma's database doesn't record the dates people join or renew.

After a little thought, however, she realises that she can make a pretty good estimate from the accounts. By totalling up the amount of membership fees paid in each week the pattern becomes clear immediately. This gives the Committee the information they wanted; they don't need the exact membership figures, and it's not worth the extra effort of finding out.

Where to start

An exercise in selecting information more efficiently can be carried out for just one individual or for a small team. Sometimes it may be appropriate to do it as part of a major exercise for a whole organisation. However, that's quite an ambitious undertaking, not to be embarked on lightly. It's often best to start out at the pinch points, by asking:

- who is feeling particularly overwhelmed?
- can they do anything on an individual level?
- which information that we don't have do we desperately need?

If you start off in this way, the only thing to be wary of is that you don't just push the problem around within your organisation. One person might manage to offload a great pile of their incoming information, but if they do this at the expense of someone else, the organisation has not gained.

This is where the manager has an important role. When encouraging staff to cut down their incoming information, or to restructure the information they have so that it is more use to them, they must not be allowed a completely free hand. Either direction from the top or, preferably, negotiation with their colleagues, should ensure that they really do make decisions that will benefit individual staff members and the organisation in general.

Example 9 Changing the way you get information

Maureen is the administrator in a disability charity. She maintains a central card index of all the other voluntary organisations they are in contact with, even just occasionally. Whenever a change of address notice comes through she updates the cards. She also scans incoming magazines and newsletters and notes any changed details on her card index as they are announced. However, the card index is really only a back-stop. It isn't used very often, as most of the staff keep their own records of the organisations they deal with most frequently.

During a supervision session with Sheila, the Office Manager, Maureen mentions that updating the index is taking time she doesn't really have. Sheila very gently suggests scrapping the card index completely and buying printed directories from NCVO, the local CVS and the local disability network instead. Although these won't be quite as up to date as the card index, they will fulfil the back-stop role admirably. If anyone does happen to come across out of date details in one of the directories they can just write the correction into the book. After a bit of persuasion, Maureen agrees.

How to cut down the information you receive

To start applying an information strategy, it is usual to ask 'What information is necessary for this job?', then to work out where it is best acquired. A more rough and ready approach – which will do well here – is to review the information which actually arrives, and ask 'Do I need this to do my job?'.

If you don't need the information, then you need to work out how to stop it coming. It could be as easy as cancelling a subscription; but it might involve asking your colleagues to provide you with information in a different way, or reorganising the way information coming into the organisation is handled.

You also have to be careful about defining 'need'. On the one hand, be pretty ruthless. Think 'What is the worst that could happen if I didn't have this information? And how likely is that to happen?'. Even if the potential consequences are quite harmful, they may be so unlikely that the risk is worth taking. But on the other hand it is possible to get too carried away and cut off so much that stop being aware of what is happening in the wider world.

Even if you do need it, you have to assess whether the way you get each kind of information is actually the best way. Do you have to wade through a lot of irrelevant material to find a few bits that you really do need? Does the information come in continuously in small amounts, whereas you need it only occasionally? There may well be alternatives that are worth considering.

Practical exercise

Make a list, or even a set of piles on a clear desk, of the information that arrives during, say, one typical week. Include telephone calls and face-to-face contacts as well as paper, faxes and e-mails. Then take a good hard look at it all, and try to work out how you can cut it down. It might help to divide the material at this state into two piles.

- **Category 1** – things I subscribe to or receive as part of a general mailing, that are written for a general audience and maybe even arrive unsolicited;
- **Category 2** – things directed specifically to me.

Now, using the suggestions below, work out how you can reduce the items in category 1 by 10%, or more if you can. Set aside time a month from now to review your decisions and see whether anything needs reinstating, or whether there are more items you could cut out.

Meanwhile, get a colleague to help you get to grips with category 2.

Category 1: general mailings and unsolicited material

First, ask why you receive these materials. What benefit does the organisation get from you receiving them? Do you need to read them when you get them, or are they just for reference? How much of each magazine or mailing is relevant? Do you get the same information from more than one source? If you miss the information would you know? If so, could you get the information at a later date?

You have several options at this stage.

- Cancel the subscription.
- File the material without reading it (or get someone else to file it without it even crossing your desk), because you know it is likely to be needed in future. (But be realistic, keeping things 'just in case' is *not* a good idea.) !
- Extract the most relevant bits when it arrives *and throw away the rest* without reading it (or possibly pass it on to someone else in the organisation to whom they are relevant).
- Skim-read to pick out the four or five most important points, and mark the item as read – don't try to go back to the boring bits later.

It's a reasonable rule of thumb that if something remains unread for more than about three months, it's probably lost its immediate relevance. (After all, the organisation has survived so far without knowing what's in it.) Either throw it away or, if absolutely necessary, file it for reference.

Don't be afraid to cancel subscriptions. Many organisations' mailings are not well thought out. Even if they sometimes contain useful information, if it's hard to find, it may not be worth it. Or you may have subscribed in the past when the material was more relevant to you than it is now.

If you find it hard to file items or throw them away without reading them, just in case you are missing something, you may find it useful to remind yourself of all the similar material that you never even see. *All* information coverage is a compromise between completeness and the time available. Think of this exercise as redrawing the boundary slightly in favour of time.

You may also find it useful to think about where your genuinely creative, innovative and vital information does come from. Could you replace one of your existing sources of less useful information with one which covers similar ground but in a more productive way?

Category 2: material directed specifically to you

Because they are directed specifically to you, items in this category can be harder to ignore. However, that does not necessarily make them relevant. Time-management techniques can be helpful here. The three options are:

- do;
- dump; or
- delegate.

The most important thing is to handle the item as few times as possible. Put it in one of the above categories the first time you pick it up if possible. If it is in the 'do' group, try to make a realistic assessment of when you will do it. If you know you cannot do it today, put it in a file for tomorrow, or next week, so that you don't handle it again until there is a reasonable chance of taking the required action. See Example 15 for more on this.

Reducing the amount of category 2 material is also possible. Try getting your colleagues to summarise information before they give it to you, or at least to highlight the bits you need to attend to. Don't immediately reply to e-mail messages unless *you* decide that it's important to do so. You will gradually educate your regular correspondents not to expect an instant response.

Example 10 Less is more

Andy is a development worker in a community development agency with a staff of 15. Like most members of staff, he finds in his pigeon-hole every month a six-page printout of the latest figures comparing spending against the budget. From this he can find out which of his budget headings are over- or under-spent. However, to find this information he has to wade through pages of information that applies to other staff, and over which he has no control.

When Andy raises this problem at a staff meeting, Carol, the finance officer, says that it just seemed easiest to print off a copy of the monthly figures for everyone. However, she agrees to set up her spreadsheet so that the figures relating to budgets held by each member of staff can be consolidated into one place. Once Carol has done the work of setting up the spreadsheet, it takes her no further effort each month to print off a single page for each member of staff like Andy, showing only the figures relevant to them. If Andy wants to know how other people are doing he can ask – it's not a secret – and once or twice a year the whole organisation has a session on the budget. But in the meantime, Andy just gets one, relevant sheet of paper each month, making it more likely that he will pay attention to it and actually notice if he is in danger of going over budget.

In this case, less information not only means less work and less paper; it also holds out the possibility of better decision-making because crucial information is less likely to be overlooked.

'They keep sending me these great piles of paper. Do you think they'll stop when they realise I don't read them?' Greg Dyke, recently appointed BBC Director General, quoted in The *Guardian*, 15 November 1999.

No one has to know everything

It is said that one issue of a Sunday newspaper contains more information than someone living in the seventeenth century would read in their lifetime. The days when one person could be knowledgeable in the detail of a wide range of different subjects are gone. There is so much information available that no one can possibly know everything.

Pressure point

I sometimes panic that we might look stupid because we missed some vital piece of information.

When everything moves so fast, and even in the voluntary sector organisations jostle for 'competitive advantage', it's important to be up to date with a wide range of information. It could be legislative changes that affect your work, or developments in good practice. It could be knowledge of funding opportunities or local government policies.

Achieving this without overloading yourself is a delicate balancing act. Some useful approaches include:

- rewarding staff, volunteers or management-committee members who share useful 'intelligence';
- choosing carefully which information sources to subscribe to;
- identifying where you need expert help;
- knowing who the experts are, and checking with them from time to time;
- networking intensively with people in other organisations.

Specialising

The way to achieve enough depth of knowledge without becoming over-loaded is to specialise, operating on a 'need to know' basis, and to collaborate with others. Decide what you, your team or your organisation can be expert in, then work out where you can tap into other people's expertise in other areas.

- You could have a **formal agreement** with another organisation that you will each take an area to specialise in and share your information as required.

- There are many technical areas where it almost certainly makes more sense to **buy in expertise when you need it**: law, personnel matters, and information technology are some of the more obvious ones. It may even be worth paying a retainer to someone to alert you to new developments, and perhaps to come in once a year to review your practice.
- If your organisation is a member of a **local or national network**, some of this expertise should be available from that source. If not, why are you a member? Is there another network that would provide you with the support you need?
- **Within your organisation** you should operate in the same way. If one person does a lot of work developing model standard letters or information sheets to cope with particular situations, it should be a matter of course that they share them with others.

This approach fits well with the way people like to work. Research has shown that people faced with a question they can't answer generally prefer to ask someone else rather than looking it up for themselves. Everyone has their favourite 'guru' on whom they rely for expertise in certain areas. Even when the person you first ask can't help, they may well suggest someone else, who suggests someone else, until the right person is found. It can be useful to formalise this to some extent, and make it an explicit organisational policy.

It is important that the two sides to this approach go hand in hand: you may decide not to bother being an expert in a particular area, but that doesn't mean that you should ignore it. If it's important, then you must identify who you *are* going to rely on. You have to know that you can trust this source, and you have to know who they are so that there is no delay in contacting them in an emergency.

Example 11 Selective specialisation

Corinna is the Information Officer of the North Wessex Council for Voluntary Service (CVS). She receives queries covering a very wide range of topics from member voluntary organisations, but she quickly realises that she cannot be an expert in all of them. After some thought, and an analysis of the types of questions that come in, she decides that she should specialise in the areas of constitutional issues, charity status and fundraising. She devotes most of her resources budget to building a library of up-to-date material in these areas, and subscribes to specialist journals as well as investing in relevant computer software.

So what happens when she gets a question on personnel, or IT, or health and safety, or insurance? If it is straightforward she may be able to answer it from the more general reference works that she has to hand. But if it is too complex for her to deal with alone, she turns to one of her

---

'experts'. On personnel matters, for example, she has developed a good working relationship with Tracey, her opposite number in the Rural Community Council. Although it's not written down anywhere, they each know that they can ask the other for help. Corinna can ask Tracey if she gets stuck on a personnel matter, while Tracey uses Corinna's expertise on constitutional issues. Every so often, the two sit down over lunch and go through recent developments in their areas of expertise, so that neither is likely to get taken by surprise or appear totally ignorant when someone calls.

On IT Corinna doesn't have a single source of expertise, but every time she is in contact with a member organisation she asks them who they use. Gradually she has built up a list of people, mainly local, specialising in different areas of IT. For health and safety Corinna has decided to refer people to a specialist agency in Bristol, especially now that they have set up a very useful Web site, while insurance matters get referred to the Honorary Treasurer of the CVS who works for a large voluntary organisation where he is responsible for insurance among other things.

This example is obviously much neater than real life, but the crucial point is that, having decided that she doesn't need to specialise in certain areas, Corinna can cut down on the information she receives. She doesn't need to subscribe to a specialist personnel briefing. She can skim the general magazines she gets, and ignore anything about IT, unless she has a bit of spare time. She doesn't have to file lots of material about insurance.

Example 12 Choosing the most appropriate sources

As the chief officer of a small care organisation, Ramesh had problems keeping up to date with employment law. When he started the job he found that his predecessor had just ignored the subject, and had happily carried on using illegal contracts and out-of-date terms and conditions.

Determined to do something about this, Ramesh subscribed to an updating service for £200 a year. For this, he receives a fat ring-binder full of technical information and every month a packet in the post with some 50 new pages which have to be inserted in the right place and the old ones thrown away. Needless to say, he rarely finds time to do this immediately. Although he now has a source of information he can trust on the rare occasions when he needs to look something up, he still feels that he isn't really on top of changes to the law. Even when something in the updating package catches his eye, he sometimes isn't sure exactly how it applies to his organisation, because he isn't an expert.

Sushila, a colleague from another part of the country, faces the same problem but has solved it in a different way. She has decided that if anything really important happens she is unlikely to miss it among all the mailings she receives, not to mention the national press. What she really wants is someone to talk through issues with when they arise. Her Council for Voluntary Service employs a personnel specialist who, for a small, fixed annual fee, is available to talk through employment issues on the phone. If an organisation needs more detailed help they can buy in consultancy, again at favourable rates.

Ramesh isn't so lucky; his CVS doesn't offer an equivalent service. But he does find a local independent employment consultant who is able to offer a similar deal, and he decides to use the same approach as Sushila.It has taken him some time, but Ramesh has moved from a position of having no information at all to one where he had information but had to work too hard at it, and finally to one where he can relax in the knowledge that he doesn't have to worry at all because he knows exactly where to find help if he needs it.

Good information is rarely free, but Ramesh and his committee agree that the saving in his time and peace of mind are worth more to the organisation than the cost of the service. Ramesh decides that this has worked so well that he will try to make similar arrangements in other areas such as health and safety.

Statistics and monitoring

Funders and regulatory agencies ask for far more information nowadays than they used to. Management committees are under more pressure than ever to demonstrate that they are doing their job properly, which means asking the staff for more information. Members and supporters want more evidence of how their contributions are being spent. All this means that organisations have to produce more and more statistics and other information to monitor their work. There is a danger of being swamped with bureaucracy, leaving less time for 'real' work.

There are several ways in which you can make your collection of statistical information as efficient as possible.

■ Try to base your statistics on information that you would collect anyway, rather than giving yourself extra work. See Example 14.

- If you need to do something like client profiling for your funders, consider whether this could be done on a sample basis – two days a month or every tenth client, for example – rather than for everyone.
- Try to be consistent in the way you present information. For example, if your financial year is April to March, don't report usage statistics for January to December unless you have a really good reason.
- Plan your information system so that information from which statistics will have to be prepared is stored together, rather than scattered around.

Example 13 Collect statistics which suit your needs

Martin runs a small youth advice agency, and has to report his clients' ages in bands (0–15, 16–17, 18–20 etc.) to his funders. He decides to design his enquiry record form with a box to tick for each band, rather than asking the actual age. That way, he has less work to do when it comes to working out the totals. Once the case is closed he never needs to update the client's age.

Joy, on the other hand, is the membership secretary of a youth organisation. She inherits an application form for membership with age-band boxes. However, when she enters this on her database she finds that there is no way of knowing when someone moves from one band to another and becomes eligible for a different category of membership. So she redesigns the form to ask for date of birth (with an explanation of why she needs the information).

When designing questionnaires or forms for collecting information, consider how you will use the results.

- Design the form or database on which you collect information so that it feeds directly into the statistics you want. See Example 13.
- Design forms carefully, especially if they are to be filled in by clients or members of the public rather than staff. Always test a form with people who have not been involved in drawing it up, to ensure that the questions mean what you intend them to mean, that there is enough space for each answer, and that the flow through the form is coherent.
- Don't give yourself more work than you have to. For example, if you get people to evaluate a service by scoring or multiple choice it is easier to turn that into simple statistics than if you ask for written comments (which is also more work for them, and less likely to be done). To allow for individuality, have a space for additional comments at the end, or if you can identify the person go back to those whose replies are anomalous.

- Don't use too many different techniques on one form (e.g. in general don't mix tick-boxes and options to be circled; don't score some things on a numerical scale and others by description such as 'poor', 'average', 'good').
- Don't give people too many options: it's harder for them to fill in, and more work for you to collate and report on. A five-point scale (or four if you deliberately don't want people to choose a middle option) will probably give you as much information as you need, without forcing people to puzzle over whether their feelings are best represented by six or seven out of ten.
- Ask fewer, simpler questions. 'Would you recommend this training course to others?' may be all you need to know. You can offer 'Yes', 'No' and 'Yes, but only if ... '

Good form design is not easy. Take advice or read up on it if you have to do it a lot.

Example 14 Keeping it simple

If you know that your funders are interested in which part of the city your clients come from, can you base that information on postcode rather than something more esoteric like council wards? Nearly everyone knows their postcode, and you are likely to collect it anyway when you get people's addresses. Finding wards on the other hand is likely to involve you in a lot more work, as you would have to ask it separately and many people don't know. If possible, persuade your funders that they would prefer accurate data on postcodes, instead of incomplete guesswork on council wards.

When you report your findings from statistical information, consider your audience.

- A few clear figures are much easier to understand than a lot of detail. For most people it is enough to know that the total number of cases, visitors, clients or whatever went up or down, and possibly the two or three categories that moved most. Have the full details available separately for those few who really need them. Watch how the financial news is reported on TV for a good example.
- Portray statistics graphically whenever possible. People find it much easier to understand the main points or trends that way.

Financial information

The accounts are often seen as a regrettable necessity. Most people would agree that it is important to know how much money your organisation has spent, to ensure that you don't go overdrawn at the bank, and to pay staff on time. However, the time and effort that goes into the book-keeping and preparation of accounts can also be used in many other ways to help managers and other decision-makers.

Part of the problem is that the format in which most voluntary organisations' accounts have to be prepared in order to comply with the law doesn't lend itself well to more creative use. It is not just a matter of preparing a cash-flow – predicting future spending patterns – as well as historical accounts. An up-to-date cash-flow projection can be essential. However, following the principles outlined above, this should often be the province of only the book-keeper or accountant. No one else needs to see all the figures. What managers may need to know about are the specific instances where the cash-flow projections indicate a future problem, so that they can take decisions in plenty of time.

Using accounts information in management

We have shown how staff members with budgetary responsibilities may need to be given their own specific information so that they can manage their budgets properly (Example 10 above). Where else might the organisation ask its financial team to produce information from their basic accounts that can help the managers?

One crucial area is for fundraising and preparing grant applications. With more and more funding being project-specific, it is harder than ever to cover the 'core' costs – those which are not obviously connected with a particular project. The solution is to include a share of the core costs in each funding application or appeal; but to do this, you have to know how much each project's share of the core costs amount to. For many organisations this is now second nature, but if your organisation does not already have a system for allocating these core costs in a way which convinces donors and funders, it could well be losing out, either by asking for too little, or by failing to justify the amounts requested.

Another area where the right financial information can make a difference is in spotting trends soon enough to act. If your organisation depends for part of its income on members, you may well take a snapshot of the number of members once a year, probably around the time of the annual general meeting. But the accounts probably record membership income monthly. It shouldn't take long to compare this year with the equivalent time last year, and the year before, to give you a pretty good idea of how you're doing. Publication sales may be hard to compile item by item; your stock control may not be perfect, or you may have material out on sale or return, or on bookstalls. But if you get some of your income from sales, you have a ready source of information to give you a broad picture of how you're doing.

Expenditure, too, can give you useful pointers. If the amount spent on staff travel suddenly goes up, does it mean that your outreach workers are doing more outreach and spending less time in the office? Or does it mean that a new member of staff is more flexible in their interpretation of the rules than you would like? Either way, spotting the trend is the first step in formulating the right questions to ask.

Commercial organisations are perhaps too concerned about the 'bottom line'. People running voluntary organisations are bound to be interested in far more than just the financial outcome; but using financial information to get a picture of the health of different parts of the organisation is not falling prey to commercial pressures, it's just an effective use of the information that is already at your disposal.

Re-using information

The area of accounts provides a good example of how the amount of information you have to deal with can be reduced by re-using the same information for several different purposes. The possibilities are particularly exciting when computers come into the equation. Once material is on computer, it requires relatively little effort to adapt it in many different ways, and in a properly planned system to get the computer to do a lot of the work for you – producing a wide range of labels, lists and so on automatically from a single database, or lifting figures from the accounts straight into a spreadsheet.

There are several questions you can ask yourself, before you sit down to seek out information from scratch.

- Has this been done before? Might anyone in our organisation, or even in another organisation, have something I can use at least as a starting point?
- Is this question likely to come up again? (If so, instead of answering just the immediate points, you could draft the material so that it is suitable for re-use in the future.)
- Does this question come up frequently? (If it does, you might be better off creating a more elaborate standard reply, or even getting someone to write a briefing or factsheet.)
- Can this information be used elsewhere or by someone else? Instead of just sending out a response to the person who asked for the information and filing your own copy, make sure that anyone else who may be able to benefit from your work knows what you have done.

Personal good practice

You can help yourself by adopting good practices in your personal use of information, and by encouraging others to follow them too.

Pressure point

I just can't find important information even when I know we have it somewhere.

Everyone knows that embarrassing situation when you have a vital piece of paper in your hand, then 15 minutes later you can't find it, no matter how you try. Or when:

- someone leaves, and no one can make sense of their computer files;
- a long-standing staff member asks for a copy of their employment contract, which cannot be found;
- you need to base a new course on training material you used last year, but which is now buried somewhere among other past activities;
- you remember seeing something in a magazine - but which one, and when was it?

The disappearing sheet of paper may sometimes be just one of those things, but it is easier to find information when you:

- have 'a place for everything and everything in its place';
- design your information systems around the questions you are likely to ask;
- allocate time for filing little and often;
- make sure to keep only material that is worth keeping. ✄

Organising your desk and work area

A tidy house may be the sign of a bored householder, but a tidy desk can genuinely make a difference to how you use information. Nearly everyone has been in the situation where they had a piece of paper in their hand just a moment ago, containing vital information, and now they can't find it in the sea of papers around them. Quite possibly this is just a law of nature which kicks in when you are particularly busy; but if people build flood defences and earthquake-proof buildings, why not an information-friendly desk?

The key, of course, is making sure that you keep papers on your desk only if you are currently working on them. Don't have large heaps of stuff requiring action. When you first look at something, decide when you are realistically going to be able to attend to it, and then put it somewhere appropriate. The system you devise has to work for you: it doesn't have to be elegant, but it should keep paper off your desk when you're not working on it.

If you are working on several projects simultaneously which each involve large amounts of information, find somewhere to keep the files other than on your desk. This can be a drawer in your desk, part of your filing cabinet, even a nearby table.

Example 15 A no-list system

Richard is the Manager of a small, busy organisation. He knows he is not very good at prioritising things by means of lists, so he has devised a simple system that works for him. He has three filing trays on his desk, labelled 'Review daily', 'Review weekly' and 'Review monthly'.
Everything he thinks he ought to do this week is the first of these. Things to be done this month are in the second. Really long-term things are in the third. He also has a small folder in the 'Review daily' tray for 'Today's tasks'.

When he comes in each morning he goes through the 'Review daily' tray, pulls out anything he needs to take action on today, and puts it in the folder for 'Today's tasks'. The folder sometimes also has a list of jobs that don't have a corresponding piece of paper. He then works through the folder during the day. Occasionally it is completely empty by the end of the day, and one of the things he is working on in his supervision sessions with the chair of the organisation is learning to be more realistic about how much he puts in the folder. Emptying it completely gives him a really good feeling, and is something he needs to achieve more often.

Each Monday, Richard goes through the 'Review weekly' tray, and moves everything for this week into the 'Review daily' tray. At the beginning of each month, he looks at the 'Review monthly' tray.

This system works because Richard generally has lots of tasks based around small amounts of paper: letters or messages to be answered, financial reports to look at, draft papers to read, and so on. He doesn't have much bulky material such as client files. He is also able to be at his desk often enough to check through the trays according to his set routine, ensuring that he doesn't miss things.

Longer-term projects

Richard occasionally has to work on funding applications which involve collecting a large amount of background material before he can settle down to the writing. This often sits around for days, even weeks, while other people prepare their contributions. Then there are the papers for meetings of the management committee. These accumulate over the period between meetings, and eventually get used for drawing up the agenda. Richard uses the large drawer in his desk for files like these. But of course, he mustn't forget they are there, so in his 'Review' trays he puts notes reminding him of the key dates: *Management committee agenda to go out by 12 October* or *Draft funding application must go to staff team, 1st week of March*. When these actions are due, he pulls the file out of his drawer to work on it. Meanwhile he has easy access if he needs to drop relevant papers into the file, without it cluttering his desk.

Filing

Once you have finished using papers, get them off your desk as quickly as possible. If they are to be filed, the ideal solution is to put them in the right place immediately. Little and often is a good rule with filing; if you file things straight away, you won't have to work out all over again where they belong.

Inevitably there will be times when you just need to push something out of the way in order to get on with something else urgent. The danger is that it goes into a 'filing' tray which just gets fuller and fuller, making the eventual task of dealing with it ever more daunting. Assuming that you really do need to keep it, you may be able to break the problem down into more manageable chunks.

- Perhaps have a series of smaller files: 'things to go back to other people', 'things to go into the library or reference section', 'things to be punched so that they can go into ring binders', 'financial stuff', or whatever makes sense to you.
- Try to do a little bit of filing regularly at times when you wouldn't be doing 'serious' work anyway – around each tea break, while you're waiting for someone to arrive for a meeting.

You may also benefit from reorganising your system. Look at the items which hang around un-filed for a long time; is it because it's hard to know where they go, or because the filing cabinet is over-full? If you make your filing harder than it need be, it's almost bound to get out of hand. (See Chapter 6 for more on this.)

'Reading' files

Finally, it is probably a mistake to have a pile of material 'for reading' on your desk. Again, try to break it into categories. If you have to read something in order to take action – review a draft report, comment on a consultation document, implement a new policy from 'head office' – don't categorise it as reading. It's a task on its own, and should take its place in your priority list alongside correspondence and projects you have initiated. If possible, the papers should be immediately put together with any other material they relate to. For example, if the policy from head office relates to your next management committee meeting, put it in the 'Next Management Committee' file straight away.

This leads on to a general principle: the fewer times you have to handle a piece of paper, the better. When you pick something up for the *first* time, decide what has to happen to it, as precisely as possible. Write on the item to remind you what you have decided. Mark or highlight anything particularly relevant the first time you read it. This will save you having to re-read the whole thing when you go back to it.

Material for reading which you categorise as less urgent – maybe magazines, briefings, bulletins, material from other organisations – can go into a reading pile if you like, provided you take a realistic look at it from time to time. Everyone has only so many hours in the week and reading, even skimming, takes time. If material is coming in at a faster rate, on average, than you can read it, your reading pile is going to grow inexorably. You can't change the laws of mathematics by wishful thinking.

Practical exercises Review your reading file and working area

1 Over a 'typical' week (not a relaxed, optimistic one) check how much reading you actually manage to do. Better yet, get someone else to check for you - they're more likely to be honest. Multiply by 40 (the number of normal working weeks in the year, allowing for holidays, sickness, crises, AGMs and the like) – and that's how much reading you can allow onto your pile. Anything above that you will have to eliminate, either by deciding you don't need the information, or by finding a different way to get it.

2 Go through your reading pile and throw away anything that is so out of date that it can no longer possibly be relevant. You may be surprised to find out just how long things can accumulate unread. Will your work really benefit from you reading something two or three years old?

3 Once a year (at least) get someone to help you make a ruthless review of your working area, to pick up on things which have been hanging around for too long, and to dispose of them. (OK it's embarrassing, but you can do the same for them.)

Organising your communications

Communication style is a very personal business. You need to work out what is best for you. However, there are a few general principles which can help both you and your colleagues.

- Don't double-up on communications. If you send a fax, don't put a confirmation copy in the post without a very good reason. Don't phone to say you're sending an e-mail; if you need to know the person has got the message, why not contact them by phone in the first place?
- If you know that someone will need information from you, make sure you give it to them so that they don't have to chase for it.
- Use consistent ways of recording each type of information. As far as possible, keep all your phone numbers in one place, and all your addresses, so that you're not hunting around all the time when you need to contact someone.
- When you take a phone message make sure you get the key information: who called, who for, when, what about, how and when to get back to them. (If it helps, use a pre-printed message pad.)
- Practise 'management by exception' for most things. Instead of reporting on everything that's happening, just point out the bits that are not going to plan, or not meeting their targets, or have changed since last time.
- Cut out all the supporting data and just give a headline. Tell people where to go for the additional material if they need it.
- Make the subject lines of your e-mails as informative as possible, to help the recipient decide how and when to respond.
- Make use of your rights under the Data Protection Act and other legislation to cut down direct marketing material.
- Remember that no one can be expert in everything, and make sure you attempt to cover only what you need to.

STORING INFORMATION

Storing information effectively is not always easy. Professional librarians spend a considerable amount of their time working out how to classify, store and catalogue their material, and then making sure that it gets put back in the right place once it has been borrowed or used. Most people's working areas are a testimony to the problems that can arise:

- papers all over the place because there is 'nowhere to put them';
- heaps of papers 'waiting to be filed';
- key documents disappearing under a mountain of material that has arrived more recently;
- papers 'filed' away that can never be found again;
- messages stuck on top of things, in the hope that they get noticed;
- out-of-date lists of phone numbers and collections of business cards.

All these are not merely inconvenient; they actually prevent the work of the organisation from getting done. The solution is partly to encourage people to learn better information-handling habits, but mainly for the organisation to take a lead in setting up a clear framework which allows people to put their information in the most suitable place.

Principles of information storage

In order to comply with the principles of effective information management, there are three key principles to designing a good filing system, or other way of storing information.

1 Make it simple and intuitive.
2 Think of who will use it and what for.
3 Gear the design around the output.

Make it simple and intuitive

In a simple and intuitive system you will, for example:

- ensure that the information people need most often is placed in the most accessible positions.
- make it easier to use the files by having categories which people don't have to puzzle over, and which leave the least scope for different interpretations.

- label files with names that mean something in people's work, rather than arbitrary numerical or alphabetical codes.
- avoid complicated systems of colour-coding unless you are sure there is no danger of them breaking down. (Will there always be a stock of those purple file folders?)
- build in features which can guide people along if they have to do things in a particular order.

Think of who will use it and what for

- Does the system need to be accessed in a hurry, while someone is on the phone?
- Can the information be used and then replaced, or are people likely to need to keep it on their desks for days at a time?
- Would it matter if other people then couldn't use the same information?
- Does the information have to be taken out of the office – to meetings or on home visits, for example? Or might people have to use it from home?

Pressure point

I don't know the best way to store the material we generate.

Every organisation generates its own information – minutes of meetings, case and client records, materials used on training courses, background research for newsletters or information sheets, staff and volunteer records, financial records, funding applications, reports, plans, memos.

Sometimes the problem is just knowing the best way to record or file things. In other cases cross-referencing may be the problem: should training material and background research all be in the same place? if not, how do you relate one to the other?

Some of the answers in this area include:

- designing your information systems around the questions you are likely to ask;
- training your staff to contribute less to each other's information overload;
- keeping only material that is worth keeping;
- using computers where it is genuinely beneficial.

Gear the design around the output

Taking the output into account means always thinking what the information will mainly be used for. The key question is: 'What question will I be asking when I use the system?' If you regularly need to report on your activities in the form of statistics, it probably makes more sense to keep all the statistics in one place, rather than scattered through a large number of project files. If people often phone in to find out about the nearest branch of your organisation to them, that suggests perhaps holding the information on a map, rather than alphabetically by county – even pinning little flags to the map with the branch's name or the contact's phone number. More detailed information might then be held somewhere else.

An example can show these principles in operation, but every case is different; there is no substitute for thinking analytically about the way your organisation needs to use information.

Example 16 Redesigning a filing system

Jack has just been appointed as a specialist trainer within his organisation to provide training for other organisations. He finds that his predecessor has kept their records in files for each client organisation. In each file are copies of the course programme, handouts, correspondence, publicity material and invoices. On the computer, the same approach has been taken, with a subdirectory for each client, holding copies of all the material relating to them. Background information on the topics covered in the training is supposed to be separate, but over time some of it has crept into the files relating to particular courses.

Jack isn't happy with the situation. While the system is certainly simple and reasonably intuitive, it doesn't give enough weight to the way the information is used and, most importantly, re-used. What happens when he wants to run another course on the same topic? How can he find the right exercises and handouts if they are scattered all over the place? How will he know which is the most recent of several similar documents?

The filing cabinets are filling up with many examples of similar but slightly different course materials. And when someone asks 'How many people have you trained on such and such a topic?' Jack has to trawl through masses of paper to find the significant details.

How should he store the information? First Jack looks at the information involved:

- background information on the topic;
- course programmes and descriptions;
- handouts, overheads and other material used on the day;
- correspondence with each client organisation about where and when

the course is to be held, what facilities are required, and who is attending;

- publicity material for each course produced by or for the client organisations;
- invoices and other financial details.

After consideration, Jack devises a new system:

- one set of 'historic' files for clients;
- another set of files for background material on topics, supplemented by a set of box files arranged by the same topics for books and larger documents;
- a third set of files for copies of training materials.

These file systems are mirrored on the computer, where there is one subdirectory for standard letters to clients and one per topic for training materials.

When a new client books a training course, Jack runs off a standard checklist and opens a new 'current' file, using a clear folder so that the checklist inside can be easily seen. This checklist allows him to see at a glance whether all the arrangements have been finalised, whether the contract has been sent out and received back after signing, whether the handouts have been prepared, and so on. Inside the folder goes all the correspondence, maps of how to reach the venue and, eventually, copies of the programme and the handouts that have been designed for that specific client, plus any background material being taken on the day (if it will fit).

After the course, once the invoice has been paid, Jack's final task is to break down the contents of the 'current' folder.

- Background material goes back where it came from.
- Most of the correspondence is thrown away, but in the 'historic' file for that client goes the checklist, plus a list of participants. If it's available, a summary of the evaluations might also go here. At any time in the future, it will be easy to go through these thin client files and work out which course was held when, how many people attended, and what they thought of the course. Invoices are not kept here, but in the finance system.
- Copies of the timetable, handouts and exercises then go in the relevant 'training materials' folder. However, Jack first considers whether these should be regarded as additional materials, or updates which can replace what is already in the folder. If legislation has changed, for example, the old material is no longer relevant and

should be thrown away. However, an exercise developed particularly for that client might be kept, in case it could be used in future.

On the computer, correspondence is kept only as standard letters. Individual letters are printed (with a copy for the 'current' file if absolutely necessary) but not saved. Training materials are divided into course-specific (such as a timetable) which are saved under the name of the client, and general, where just the latest version of each hand-out, overhead or exercise is stored.

This way, for very little effort, Jack has a system which stores the minimum amount of paper required, and makes it as easy as possible to get access to what is needed when past courses are being analysed or future ones planned.

The most important point here is that this example is as much concerned with *process* as with *structure*. When we design an information system, what happens to the information is just as important as where it is kept; you can't make sense of the one without the other.

The structure of a filing system

There are essentially two different ways to structure a filing system. You can make it:

- easy to put things in; or
- easy to get things out.

An example of the first is a correspondence file where each piece of correspondence is merely filed in date order as it is received and replied to. Putting items in is just a matter of opening the file and adding them to the top. However, if you ever need to go back and find a particular letter – perhaps while someone is on the phone asking why they didn't get a reply – you may have serious problems finding what you are looking for.

An example of the second approach would be membership records where everything to do with a particular member is filed in one place: their application form, subscription records, attendance at training courses and meetings, correspondence, and so on. Putting this information in may take some time: you have to find the right file, for a start; you also may have to transfer information from other sources (e.g. the attendance sheet from an event).

However, if you want to know the answer to anything about your organisation's dealings with that person, it's all there in one place.

A computer database almost always takes the second approach, since you generally end up having to transfer information from paper records of one kind or another onto the computer. Provided it's well designed, however, the power you then have to get at the information may well be worth the effort. (A poorly designed system, on the other hand, may give you the worst of both worlds: time-consuming to put things in *and* awkward to get them out.)

Pressure point

We keep getting asked for information about our work that we can't easily provide.

Funders are under increasing pressure to justify the value of the money they give, so they tend to ask for more and more data on the organisations they fund. Each funder, of course, asks for different information, and you can end up spending a lot of time responding. Worse, when you don't have the information to hand, you have to spend a lot of time digging it out and collating it. Where the information is too hard to get, or non-existent, you may even be tempted to invent it: beware – this is very risky, as many organisations have found to their cost.

To avoid these problems:

- design your information systems around the questions you are likely to be asked;
- clarify with the funders what they need to know, and if possible negotiate for them all to accept the same information;
- monitor and evaluate your activities at an appropriate level – not too often or in too much detail;
- use information as intensively as possible, so that information collected for one purpose can also be used for others.

Which system to use?

Whether an 'easy in' or 'easy out' system is likely to be most appropriate in each case will be determined mainly by your answers to the questions of who is going to use it and what output is likely to be required. If you can't rely on people to cope with a complex system, perhaps because they don't use it very often, make sure it is easy to get things into the right place, even if it then takes time to find them again. If the priority is getting specific information out in a hurry, the time taken to file things properly in the first place may well be worthwhile.

There is a half-way house which might help people who need an 'easy-out' system but find they are always falling behind with their filing. For each detailed section of the filing system, an additional section is created into which everything is first sorted. Once you have identified the general topic that applies, it is much quicker to put everything – unsorted – into the relevant place. At a later stage this can be distributed into the more detailed sections, either at a planned time or when information needs to be retrieved.

The advantages of this system are that:

- filing is less likely to build up to the point where it becomes overwhelming;
- items are much easier to find, as they are in smaller quantities, and near their proper location.

The only extra thing that has to be remembered is that if you go to look something up you need to check in the general file as well as the detail file. Of course, that's a good opportunity to take a few minutes sorting the general file and putting away everything in it, not just the items you are interested in.

Example 17 An easy-in system

In our office we have a collection of street maps for different cities that staff have to visit. The most important thing is to get them back into the filing system when they have been taken out, so there are just two library boxes, labelled 'A-K' and 'L-Z'. Within each box the maps are not in alphabetical order, but it doesn't take long to go through the relevant box to find the right map before setting out on a journey.

Example 18 An easy-out system

Roger works for a development organisation which provides a range of services to local community groups. The organisation runs training events for staff, volunteers and committee members from their member organisations; it arranges people on secondment from local companies and other experienced managers to coach and support the staff, and it gives advice on policies and procedures.

Roger has to decide in principle whether to organise the files by member organisation or by activity. The 'easy-in' approach would be by activity. There would be a set of files for training events, for example. Each time there was an event, the course programme, the attendance sheet and other relevant details would go into a file. Another set of files would cover model policies, one for constitutions, one for equal opportunities and so on.

However, Roger realises that what he really needs to know about is the whole range of contacts his organisation has had with each client. When he gets a phone call from the organisation, or when he is discussing a possible placement of a secondee, he wants to be able to see which training events they have sent people to, which policies they have worked on, and any past history of secondments, as well as general enquiries and correspondence. He also needs to be able to see their annual membership renewal form, firstly to know whom he is talking to, but also to check that their payments are up to date.

As a result, Roger decides to organise the files by organisation. This means that each time there is a training event, for example, he has to take the attendance details and update a sheet in each organisation's file, to show who attended which course on which date. When he discusses a secondee, all the correspondence goes into the organisation's file – which means he has to make copies of the letters, or make a note in the file for the company offering the secondment, to make sure that he keeps track of all his dealings with them.

This all takes more work at the time, but Roger decides it is worth it because he has all the information he needs instantly available when he needs it.

Where should things be kept?

There are four guiding principles for where information should be kept.

1 **Don't keep the same kind of information in too many different places**. If you have regularly used phone numbers on a printed list, in a computerised contact-database, on business cards pinned to the wall, in directories and in your diary, the chances are you'll spend far too long looking for them.

2 **Label everything properly**. For your own purposes you can sometimes get away with knowing that a certain piece of information is in that particular green folder, but as soon as you need to share information with others, doing without clear labels is disastrous.

3 **Keep things near where they are needed**, if possible. It usually makes sense to keep phone directories near the telephone, computer manuals near the computer, and so on. If you normally need to use sources of information together, keep them together: cheque books and bank statements, funding applications and statistics about your work, all the papers which have to be taken into account in preparing the agenda for a meeting.

4 **Keep the things you need most often nearest to hand**. It is worth trying to reserve space near people's desks, in prominent filing cabinets or on easily accessible shelves for things that have to be handy. Every so often you may want to review the situation: all that material on the Single Regeneration Budget – could we move it to make space for the topics we're now dealing with most often?

Example 19

Jake is responsible for managing two minibuses at his community centre. How and where should he keep the paperwork that relates to them? There are three main types of material: related to the vehicles themselves (insurance, maintenance records, MOT, tax and so on), related to the drivers (who has been tested and is registered to drive which vehicle), and related to bookings and payments (which groups have booked for when, and whether they have paid).

The first decision Jake makes is that all the material relating to each vehicle should be together. When the tax has to be renewed, he needs the MOT and insurance documents. When he's doing the budget and working out charges, he needs all the information on how much he has spent to keep each vehicle on the road. Although some of the material could be with other finance documents and the insurance could be with buildings insurance, this arrangement would make life far too

---

complicated, and he would be forever hunting around for some vital piece of data.

This material isn't required very often, however, so Jake puts it in the normal filing cabinets, using the 'half-way house' system described in the previous section. There is one file for each vehicle, but another file for unsorted vehicle-related material. When he renews the insurance, the policy goes into the 'unsorted' file until he needs to transfer it into the file for the particular vehicle. A final file contains relevant information that is not related to either specific vehicle, such as minibus seat-belt regulations.

He could keep the information on bookings in the same place, but instead he decides that it needs to be near the phone. When people ring in, he wants to be able to tell them straight away whether a minibus is free when they want it. So he prepares charts showing a whole week for one vehicle. He prints a blank one off the computer whenever he needs it, and has them in a file near (but not on) his desk, in date order.

Information on the drivers has to be at hand when they arrive to collect a minibus. Whoever turns up, Jake needs to check that their registration to drive the vehicle is up to date. So he keeps that information by the door to the yard, together with the keys and log book that have to be issued whenever a vehicle is taken out.

Principles of filing

Getting your filing system to work effectively depends on having a sound system and then making sure that it is properly followed. The two are mutually supportive: one of the attributes of a good system is that it is relatively easy to operate properly. If your system does have to be complex, for whatever reason, documenting it and training other staff to use it become more important issues. The rest of this section outlines the main points to consider.

- **Choose a suitable classification system, the simpler the better**, other things being equal. Classification can get extremely technical, the preserve only of qualified information specialists. A few guidelines for everyday use can be found later in this chapter.
- **Ensure that people understand** the reason for seeking consistency and the benefits they will obtain from complying.
- **Don't mix very large and very small documents in one place**, as the small ones will get lost and/or damaged. Options include: two different places, such as a library box and a file folder; pasting very small items onto larger sheets

(useful for small newspaper cuttings); placing small items inside a clear plastic folder within the main file.

- **Don't use paper clips in your permanent files**. They *always* detach themselves from the right papers and catch onto ones that don't belong. If information belongs permanently together (for example receipts with a petty cash form), use staples. Treasury tags or bulldog clips, or putting a set of papers inside something else, are temporary alternatives to the dreaded paper clip.
- **Don't let your files get too big**. The advice in an old civil service manual to consider splitting a file once it has six items in it may be extreme, but it is always worth considering sub-dividing sooner rather than later. Provided the subdivisions make sense – by topic, by date or alphabetically – it will make both filing and retrieval easier.

Ordering items within files

Decide whether items are to be ordered within each set and within each file. If so, it is crucial to be consistent. For a small set of information, it may not be worth the effort to get it in order. A collection of half a dozen books, each with a distinctive cover, doesn't often benefit from being in alphabetical order. On the other hand, a set of client files probably should be in alphabetical order.

Take care to file accurately. If a file is out of order even by a few places it will be very difficult to recover it when you need it.

If **ordering items by date**, it is normal to have the oldest at the back, newest at the front. New material is therefore added at the front of the file. Occasionally you may want a file to start at the beginning, with the oldest material. If you do this, make sure you alert everyone using the file – ideally with a prominent notice on the file itself.

If **ordering alphabetically**, decide how to treat 'The', the name of your town, and other common starting words. Once decided, ensure everyone knows and sticks to the system. If in doubt, use one of the tried and tested systems, such as that used in the telephone directory (which is usefully explained in the opening pages of each directory).

If **ordering material by subject**, section labels are particularly important. Every file must have on it all the information required to get it back to its right place – i.e. the section it belongs in as well as its title. You should also make sure that the sections are ones which the users will feel comfortable with, and which are mutually exclusive. Otherwise it is inevitable that people will put material which belongs together in different places.

Methods of information storage

It is possible to spend an enormous amount of money on fancy storage equipment and supplies. Unless the need is genuine, an expensive system can easily become a white elephant. However, it is worth using a range of containers appropriate to the contents, rather than forcing everything into the same system. You should at least consider the following types of storage.

File folders are designed to live in filing cabinets or hanging files (not on people's desks or on the floor). They are suitable for short documents, mainly in A4 format. Their main advantage is that you can put individual documents in, or take them out, without taking out the whole folder as well.

Document wallets can live alongside file folders, but have the advantage that when you take them out, the contents are less likely to fall out. They are suitable, therefore, generally for short documents that have to be taken out of the office to meetings.

Ring-binders (and their big cousins, **lever-arch files**) take up more space, and are usually best kept on a shelf. They have the great advantage of keeping everything in order, and they can easily be subdivided with numbered or coloured dividers. Items can be put into or taken out from any point in the file. They are useful for working papers – this month's finances, for instance – and material that has to be updated, such as policies or directories. They are not usually a good idea for long-term storage, as they take up unnecessary space.

Library boxes (or **magazine files**) have to go on shelves, and are mainly useful for documents that can stand upright by themselves, especially if they don't have a spine that identifies them. The label on the box tells you where to find what you are looking for. These are useful for reference material, reports, magazines, catalogues and booklets. If you want to combine shorter documents with longer ones, rather than having a library box and a file covering the same subject, the short items should be protected inside a wallet of some kind within the library box.

Index-card boxes are useful for small quantities of regular information – names and phone numbers, identification numbers and service details for office equipment, indexes to large collections of material. They are quick to access, and impose no limitation on what you write: even though most cards in a set might have names and numbers, you can put messages to yourself in any format (e.g. 'contact this person via...'). Despite their speed of access and flexibility, index cards have been replaced for most people by computer databases.

File trays are *not* suitable for storage. They should only contain information that is currently being worked on.

The use of **computer databases** is such a big topic that it is covered separately in Chapter 11.

Classification

Why is classification necessary?
All information systems have to be classified; that's what makes a 'system', rather than just a heap. Classification fulfils two functions: it makes sure that material which belongs together gets placed together, and it makes it possible to find what you are looking for with the minimum of effort.

With paper documents, for simplicity, classification is usually related to storage – material is located on the shelves or in the filing system in the same order as its primary classification. Computers, however, lend themselves to much more flexibility, and to multi-dimensional classification. An organisation might be classified both by a range of functions and its location, for example, something which is hard to do on paper without a lot of tedious cross-referencing and indexing.

Approaches to classification
Classification can be a highly skilled and technical process. If you are setting up a system which is to be used for a large, permanent collection of information, or by a lot of people, or by the public, it is almost certainly worth getting professional advice.

Depending on the topic, you may find that a suitable classification system already exists. If so, this can be a very cost-effective option. An important advantage is that it may make it much easier to share and exchange information with other organisations which classify their material using the same system. Check with other organisations in your field to avoid reinventing the wheel – but before you lift someone's scheme without asking, do be aware that classification systems may be copyright. You also need to be sure that the system really does fit your needs. Does it cover all the topics you are interested in? Does it go to the right level of detail, neither too broad nor too complex? Does it use terminology you are comfortable with?

Smaller systems

With less formal systems the expense of using an expert cannot usually be justified, and a do-it-yourself approach is the only option.

- **Make sure that the terms you use are unambiguous**, and that there is no obvious overlap between different headings.
- Wherever possible **use terms that will be easily understood** by the users.
- Where there is more than one common description for the same idea, you may need to **specify 'preferred' terms** and direct users to them. For example, you probably don't want to have both 'computers' and 'information technology' as headings. When you have decided which one you prefer, you may need to make an entry that says something like 'Computers: *see Information Technology*'.
- It's perfectly acceptable to **have different levels of detail, depending on your interests**. An organisation dealing with cancer, for example, may need general headings for related illnesses and conditions, but a lot of very detailed headings for different types of cancer and issues surrounding it.
- **Stick to no more than two or three levels of heading** (more than this tends to confuse people). You may be on the wrong track if you have entries such as: 'Kitchen equipment: Feeding equipment: Cutlery: Spoons' in your directory of items for people with disabilities. Cut out at least one of the general headings, and get down to the term people are most familiar with as quickly as possible.
- **Try to avoid catch-all headings such as 'General'**. It's all too easy to find yourself classifying far too many items as 'General', only to find that they are never used because no one ever thinks of looking there. If you really find that none of the existing headings are suitable, you may need to create one that actually describes the item properly. For example, a review of different classification systems would be better in 'Classification: comparative reports', rather than 'Classification: general'.

An archive and destruction policy

How do you know when it is time to throw things away? How much do you hold onto 'just in case'? Without getting too elaborate, it is well worth establishing organisation-wide guidelines on how long information should be kept, and when it can be thrown away. This ensures that you do keep things that you have to, and protects people who throw stuff away against accusations of over-enthusiasm.

What should be kept?

First you need to determine your legal and contractual position. Certain company documents have to be kept indefinitely, by law. Personnel information may have to be kept for a long time; so may anything connected with insurance, in case a claim arises in future. Note that we say 'personnel information', not personnel files. Your archives may well not have to contain everything from your active files, and the best time to do the weeding is when the material goes into archive.

Other information that you may want to archive concerns the history of your organisation – not just minutes, reports and records of important events or transactions, but photographs and 'human interest' material. Try to strike a balance between keeping everything and frustrating future historians by throwing away too much. If possible, get an experienced, long-standing member of the organisation or someone competent at archiving to sort the material for you. Information about your own organisation is worth archiving, as no one else is likely to be keeping it.

What should be thrown away?

For out-of-date material from other organisations, historical research material, and most ephemera, your 'archive' should be the recycling bin. Ask yourself: 'Are we the first place a researcher would think of looking for this material?' 'Would they mind if they didn't find it here?' If the answer to either question is 'no', out it goes.

When should you archive?

When to move material to archives depends on the material. If your work is project-based, you may well find that much of your information has a natural life. When the project is over, the material can get archived (or binned). When a staff member leaves, their personnel file gets the treatment.

For more general material, you can schedule in regular slots – not too often, or everything is in constant upheaval, and not so infrequently that the job becomes too daunting. Weeding and archiving that takes more than a day has been left too long. You can also make archiving and weeding part of the process of using information. When you use a file, if you have time, consider whether any of the material in it has outlived its usefulness or whether that whole section of your information needs overhauling.

Pressure point

Different parts of the organisation hold conflicting information about the same topic, organisation or person.

It's no use having a wonderful information system in theory if no one uses it properly. If you decide to centralise all your contact information, or your diary, or your client information, there is no point in doing this only to find that different parts of the organisation get out of step. To avoid this:

- Decide whether you really do need a centralised system. If you do, make sure it is well designed. If you decide that a decentralised system would be more efficient (perhaps because different departments' needs don't overlap that much) you will still need to make sure that they each follow good information practice within the department.
- Don't be too ambitious. A simple system that works well is better than a complex one that doesn't. A system that achieves 80% consistency may be good enough.
- Allow people enough time to keep their part of the information up to date.
- Reward people who contribute to the centralised system and, if necessary, penalise those who don't.

SHARING INFORMATION INTERNALLY

Encouraging people to share information is one thing, but achieving this in practice is another. How often have you known: notice-boards which are never updated and never read after the first few days; meetings which take hours and leave no one any the wiser; circulating files which don't circulate, but become lost – effectively for ever.

> ### Pressure point
>
> *I don't seem to be able to get anyone in my organisation to listen.*
>
> Sharing information effectively is an important part of managing an organisation well. If people don't understand your aims and policies, or if they miss getting the information they need to do their job, they will be far less effective workers.
>
> Communication techniques could be the subject of a book in themselves, but good management of information flows within an organisation starts with a few key principles.
>
> - Tell people things in a way that they can hear, not necessarily the way you want to say them.
> - Be careful not to overload people with more information than they can take in.
> - Use an appropriate channel of communication for each message.
> - Be clear yourself about what you are saying.

Sharing information in writing

Notice-boards

The main problem with notice-boards is that they very quickly become part of the furniture. People then stop reading them. Try thinking of notice-boards not as 'for notices', but as there to *be* noticed. Notice-boards are most suitable for:

- material which people don't need often, but do need to be able to find quickly and easily, e.g. emergency phone numbers, instructions for operating nearby machinery, maps and other visual information;
- detailed factual material which people need to refer to frequently, e.g. current benefit rates, the status of each active project, places free on this month's training courses;
- material which changes frequently, e.g. weekly task lists, announcements which have immediate and short-lived effect, diary and rota information;
- material which people will see only occasionally, such as information in waiting rooms.

Notice-boards are not suitable for:

- large amounts of information, e.g. long reports or minutes of meetings (although a notice announcing that a report had finally been produced might be appropriate);
- exhortations to be better people, e.g. 'wash your own cups', 'don't forget to lock up', 'don't block the emergency exit': if people aren't remembering to do these things, they're certainly not going to obey an instruction once they have seen it every working day for months - they won't even notice it.

> Studies of the behaviour of pilots in the cockpit have shown that if vital warning signals go off too frequently they just become part of the background and get 'tuned out'. Is it any wonder that your notice-board gets ignored?

Good practice in the use of notice-boards

- Put a removal date on each item – which should rarely be more than a month ahead.
- Ensure that the notice-board is regularly weeded and updated, and that any item which has reached its removal date is removed.
- Have a clear policy on what the notice-board can be used for.

The obvious way to carry out these practices is to make it a small part of someone's job. These things won't just happen on their own.

A big secondary advantage of having tidy, well-used notice-boards is that they create a better working environment. Although it cannot be quantified, a messy, dishevelled office creates a bad impression on staff and visitors alike, and lowers morale. (However, it does not follow that everything has to be super-neat or impossibly tidy.)

Circulating files

Circulating files are an act of desperation. The idea is that material which comes into the office which might be relevant to more than one person is all regularly collected into one file. This is then passed from one worker to another. Each reads it and notes down or copies the information that they need. Then they pass it on to the next person.

It doesn't take much effort to see the flaws here. 'Why should I wade through masses of irrelevant material to pull out the stuff I need?' 'Why do I have to wait for something that might be important, while the file sits on someone else's desk?'

Don't use circulating files. Instead, you should either:

- make each person responsible for ensuring that their own information needs are met; or
- allocate to a particular person the job of directing material to the people who need it.

Magazine racks

When people realise that a circulating file doesn't work, they sometimes try a magazine rack, where all the latest issues of the magazines and other publications the organisation subscribes to are laid out. The idea is that everyone will make the time to go and read (or at least skim) the magazines they are interested in.

This is also a bad idea. Either these publications are for reference, in which case they should be filed straight away, or they are for immediate use, in which case they should go straight to the person who can use them.

Also, someone has to place the magazines in the rack when they arrive, then move them somewhere else when the next issue arrives: double-handling – to be avoided wherever possible.

Current-awareness bulletins

Sometimes there is incoming material which is likely to be relevant to a large number of staff. Given that it is highly unlikely that a notice-board, circulating file or magazine rack will get it to the right people in the most effective way, what are the alternatives?

In a small organisation it may work to make one person responsible for each incoming item. (It does not have to be a single person; the work can be shared.) As well as looking for material they need, their job is to draw attention to anything relevant to other staff, either by copying it to them or passing the publication on when they have finished. This can work if:

- the amount of material is relatively small;
- people understand properly what their colleagues are interested in; and

- they have time to do the job regularly.

If the amount of material is too big to manage in this way, the first question is obviously 'can we cut it down?' (see Chapter 5). If you really do need everything, it might be worth considering a current-awareness bulletin.

Professional information staff in large organisations often spend a lot of time producing current awareness bulletins. The idea is that incoming material is scanned, and relevant items flagged. These are then compiled into a weekly (or even daily) bulletin, summarising the item very briefly and telling those who need the detail where it can be found.

Memos

Written memos are helpful if they:

- contain short items of factual information for short-term action, e.g. 'the staff meeting has been moved to Thursday afternoon', 'the office will close on Friday next week for a filing day', 'the boiler is being serviced, so there will be no hot water for three hours on Tuesday';
- request specific action by a specific deadline, e.g. 'the material on staff changes you agreed to provide for the annual report must be on my desk by tomorrow lunchtime';
- are directed to the person or people who need to take action;
- contain genuinely important news that needs to be shared with everyone urgently and equally: 'after yesterday's interviews, Jo Bloggs has been appointed as the new chief officer, and she will start work on Monday 12 July'.

Memos are not usually productive if they:

- contain information that updates reference material, e.g. 'mileage rates are now 35p/mile for essential car users' (this is likely to be pinned up on a notice-board, then eventually buried under later material. Meanwhile the information in the office manual doesn't get changed, and so becomes out of date);
- are unspecific about what has to happen or when;
- contain general exhortations to be a good citizen, e.g. 'please remember not to prop the doors open with fire extinguishers';
- are more than a couple of sentences long;
- are sent out indiscriminately, regardless of whether people need to know what is in them or not.

If you find that you are tending to send out memos in any of these categories, it may be worth considering whether alternative means of communication would be more appropriate.

Sharing information electronically

E-mail

In many offices, e-mail has taken the place of memos. However, it can also be used for other purposes, including sending longer computer files. E-mail is notorious for contributing significantly to 'information overload'; while it can be extremely useful, it needs to be treated with care.

E-mail is suitable for:

- taking the place of memos, provided that it is used for short, practical material, clearly directed to specific people who need it (as detailed above for memos);
- urgent communication at a distance where you cannot be sure that the person at the other end will be present at a specific time;
- rapidly sharing information which is already on computer, or which the recipient will need on computer, by 'attaching' files;
- exchanging documents which are being worked on in common by two or more people.

In order to avoid some of the pitfalls, the following guidelines should be considered.

- All e-mail must be clearly identified in the subject line, so that the recipient has clear information about what is in it, and can set their own priority for reading it.
- You have to assume that e-mail is insecure. If you send confidential material there is no guarantee that it will remain confidential.
- Because it is so easy to copy and forward e-mail to multiple recipients, you need to be particularly careful to consider whether all of these people really need it. Rather than forwarding a long, complex item which is only partially relevant, and leaving them to find the bit they need, it is often better practice to extract part of the document and send it specifically to that person.
- When attaching files, pay attention to their size. If they contain more than just text, it is often worth compressing them before sending them, to reduce both your phone bill and the recipient's, or choosing a naturally compact file format (.rtf files are smaller than .doc, and .jpg are smaller than .bmp, for example).
- Because e-mail can spread viruses in certain conditions, adequate precautions must be taken.

All organisations should have (and enforce) an Acceptable Use Policy for e-mail, which might cover areas such as:

- an outright ban on offensive, illegal, libellous and pornographic material being sent or sought – with an explanation of what the organisation understands by these categories;
- guidelines on the extent to which personal use of the organisation's e-mail is permitted;
- guidelines on how the organisation interprets some of the other points above.

'An act of heresy against the religion of our time was committed yesterday. It was proclaimed that... the glut of electronic information... is not a deity but a pestilence sweeping the planet, causing illness, stress and "foolish decisions" in business.' From an article by Ed Vulliamy on a report *Dying for Information*, commissioned by Reuters, in The *Guardian*, 15 October 1996

Pressure point

Information technology bores [or terrifies] us; we know we could be using it better, but where do we start?

Most voluntary organisations nowadays rely heavily on computers, but there can be a vast difference in the way similar organisations approach their information technology. IT is a worry, because it is expensive and inherently complex. Yet it cannot be ignored. We suggest the following guidelines for good practice.

- Be clear about what your organisation is trying to achieve, and only then think where IT might fit in.
- Don't worry about being an innovator unless you really want to; tried and tested, even old-fashioned solutions can work best in some cases.
- Buy in outside expertise for many of your IT requirements.
- Ensure also that someone on the staff has responsibility for taking care of your computers, and knowing if anything is wrong.

Web sites and intranets

Because Web sites and intranets are fashionable, many organisations have gone ahead and set them up without thinking clearly about what they are best used for. Although they can be superficially cheap, given offers of 'free' Web space, the cost of setting up *and maintaining* a good site is actually significant. Before spending the money, it is essential to consider the organisation's objectives.

The difference between a Web site and an intranet is in the target audience. A Web site is available to the public, whereas an intranet uses similar technology, but is available only within the organisation.

- A Web site is suitable only for non-confidential material, whereas an intranet can, with safeguards, contain more sensitive items.
- In order to attract users, a Web site needs to be useful or interesting to them in some way, even if its main agenda is marketing the organisation. An intranet also needs to be useful, but you are not competing with others in the same way for the users' attention.
- You need to consider how people will find your site – direct advertising and links from other sites are often better than relying on Web-based indexing and search engines. An intranet can be automatically delivered to people inside your organisation.
- A Web site must take account of users' possible slow connections and a variety of Web-browser software. With an intranet you know what your users will be using and can design the site accordingly.

Some features apply equally to both types of site.

- Both are suitable for material which gets updated regularly.
- They are also suitable for archives of reference material, provided that it is well indexed.
- They are not suitable for 'current' material which doesn't get updated. There is nothing more frustrating than reading 'news' in July about something which happened in February.
- If you provide facilities for users to interact with your site by sending information or e-mail, you must make sure that you have the procedures in place to respond within the time the users would expect – a couple of days is probably the outside limit.
- Good design is crucial, to ensure that users can find what they are looking for as quickly as possible, and enjoy the experience of using the site – otherwise they will avoid using it in future.

Shared directories on the network

One of the simplest ways to share information electronically is to ensure that your computer network has an area reserved for people to store information which is intended to be shared with other people (while keeping them away from confidential material, of course). If you have a network, there are various ways in which you can consider using it to share information.

- Encourage people to store documents for common use in a shared directory.
- Train people to navigate and manipulate subdirectories so that they can find common material, even if it is not in the directory they normally use.
- Set up rules for the naming of documents so that people can easily identify the common document they want to use.
- Ensure that people know how to use passwords to protect sensitive directories and documents, while allowing several authorised people to have shared access.
- Explore the document-sharing features of common software such as your word-processor. These should be regarded as 'advanced' skills, but can be very useful when people are jointly working on the same document.

Other computer-based systems

Although an intranet is now relatively easy to set up, there are other ways of sharing information at a distance on computer. These include:

- mailing lists;
- conferencing;
- video links;
- systems which allow two computer users in different places to work on the same document at the same time.

Some of these are looked at in more detail in Chapter 11.

Pressure point

Our committee has so many legal responsibilities; it's bound to get caught out not knowing something important one day.

Keeping up to date with information in your core areas is a must. You cannot afford to be unaware of good practice or vital information for your workers or clients. But what about all the peripheral areas: personnel and employment legislation, charity law, financial regulations, health and safety, data protection... The list of areas where ignorance could be a problem seems to grow every year. Although the ultimate responsibility often rests with trustees, the board or a management committee, they rely on staff to keep an eye out for things that might affect them.

No one manager, or even several people, in a small organisation can hope to be up to date on everything. Instead, how about:

- using all your networks – local and national – to alert you to issues and changes that will affect you;
- identifying experts you can rely on, then buying in their services to get you up to date, rather than trying to do it all yourself;
- sharing resources with other organisations, so that you don't each put in effort on the same peripheral areas.

Sharing information in meetings

When to use meetings for information-sharing

Like all other aspects of managing an organisation well, meetings are more effective if those in charge are clear about the purpose. Meetings can have three main functions:

- taking decisions in an accountable, open way;
- planning future action, allocating responsibilities and reviewing progress;
- sharing information.

Before any item is put to a meeting, it is important to be clear which of these is required in this case. That may well determine whether that meeting, or any meeting, is a suitable occasion for it. Decision-making and action-planning are outside the scope of this book. What makes a meeting suitable for information-sharing?

Everyone has experienced sitting through lengthy meetings while a few people talk in detail about topics that don't affect most people in the room. It is from situations like this that meetings get their bad reputation for wasting time. However, there are ways to use meetings well for sharing information.

- Make sure that the topic is genuinely relevant to most, preferably all, of the people there. Can you arrange things so that people only have to be in the room for the items that concern them?

- Apply some of the principles discussed in Chapter 5. For example, can you give just headlines in the meeting, so that everyone is aware of the issue, but with details to follow, either in separate briefings or on paper?

- Meetings are good places to share information which is genuinely news, which affects a large number of people, where people may have questions or concerns that can immediately be dealt with, and where the factual content is limited, so that the whole issue can easily be grasped.

- They are also a good way to share information if it is important for everyone present to know that everyone else has had the same information at the same time.

- Meetings can also save time where several people have to contribute pieces of information to a whole pattern – for example synchronising diaries and arranging who is going to cover the office on which days, or represent the organisation at particular events.

Good practice in conducting meetings

There is plenty of guidance elsewhere on how to conduct effective meetings. The key role is that of Chair. From the point of view of information management, the chair should consider several points of good practice.

- Don't allow anyone to distribute written materials just before they start to talk; people will inevitably stop listening to read what they have just been given.

- Try to ensure that anyone giving a lengthy report puts the key points on paper and distributes them in advance to give people a chance to read them. If necessary, refuse to discuss papers that are brought to the meeting, or complex topics where there is nothing on paper in support.

- Make sure, though, that you don't double-up on paper and verbal presentations. There are few things more boring than listening to someone reading through a written report. The verbal presentation should add to the report and answer questions, perhaps through bullet points on an overhead, or by picking out key elements, not by going through it in detail.

- Ensure that everyone has the chance to participate, if necessary by using small groups to generate ideas and questions then having them discussed by the full group.

- Ensure that people understand when an item is on the agenda for information, and when a decision or discussion is expected.

Written information and meetings

- When giving detailed factual information in a meeting, consider whether it wouldn't be better to put the details on paper. Use the meeting to provide context and background, and to answer questions, or to share information which cannot easily be put succinctly on paper.
- Keep written papers short. If a report is more than a couple of pages long, it will gum up the meeting; try to think of a better way to cover the topic if the paper can't be cut down.
- Don't be afraid to use flip-charts and overhead projectors to share information with people in a meeting, even one which is traditionally conducted quite formally.
- Don't normally rely on minutes of the meeting as a way of sharing information. In general, keep the minutes for decisions, action points and, if necessary, reasons for the decision. Information which needs to be on record is often better presented in a separate report or paper, or shared in one of the other ways outlined in Chapter 6.

EXCHANGING INFORMATION WITH OTHER ORGANISATIONS

The time when voluntary organisations can quietly pursue their own interests without taking much notice of what others are doing is fast disappearing.

- It is increasingly necessary for organisations to participate in networks in order to keep fully up to date with all the changes which are likely to affect their work – and indeed, by disseminating information through such networks, to try to shape these changes.
- There is often pressure either to create or to participate in wider partnerships around areas of work, such as health or housing, or on a geographic basis.
- Organisations delivering services are increasingly required to do so in conjunction with other providers in the equivalent of the 'seamless' supply chains of manufacturing industries. Such practices often impose detailed specifications for record-keeping and reporting.

All of these relationships can be of vital importance. All require, to different levels of formality, the efficient exchange of information. Organisations which manage these relationships and exchanges well are far more likely to be sought after for new projects, to be listened to and to know what is going on.

The open exchange of information, based on trust, can be extremely productive. However, some organisations show the same poor attitudes to information that are present in some individuals. It is important to avoid volunteering information which may be used by more powerful and less sincere members of a partnership to take advantage of you, while you get nothing in return.

There are also changes afoot in the relationship between voluntary-sector organisations and their intended beneficiaries. In many organisations there is a shift towards user or client involvement. Alternatively, or simultaneously, the contract culture can introduce a provider-customer relationship. Whatever the cause of the change, the previous expectations of both parties are being challenged. Voluntary-sector organisations which wish to thrive need to ensure that these new information exchanges are mutually satisfactory.

Simply emphasising the importance of external information exchanges does not make them work. There are three fundamental components to managing external information successfully:

■ defining the main external organisations you are going to communicate with, and specifying why;

■ negotiating mutually acceptable norms so that people know what to expect;

■ delivering what you have agreed in a positive and impressive manner.

Defining your main external relations

Most organisations in the voluntary and community sectors work under extreme pressure. Information comes at you from all sides. It is very easy to have far more information than you can ever efficiently respond to. Meetings which don't produce results, networking for the sake of it and e-mail discussion lists which dump hundreds of messages onto your screen don't make your job easier.

So you have to set priorities. It is fairly obvious that the greatest priority is for the information you need just in order to function. But no organisation works in isolation. Even this 'essential' category is likely to include information you exchange with other organisations, such as funders, partners or suppliers. The information will only get to the right people, in the right way and at the right time if you set up systems to make sure that this happens – for example making sure that funders get the reports they have asked for on time, without having to remind you.

However, organisations also want to function in the future. At times of great change, working out what information will help you achieve this can be more challenging. You need to be scanning the environment in which you work.

A starting point is to evaluate what you are currently doing. Identify the relationships you want to continue and make sure you discuss your ideas for the future with them. Channels need to be established for two-way communication with funders, or other supporters, staff, suppliers of services and those your organisation is trying to serve. You need to tell them your views on the present, on how you think it could be improved and to listen to their experience, ideas and news. News is of particular importance. New policies in funding bodies, new products and services from specialist staff and suppliers, new projects affecting the community with which you work may all have major implications for your future.

These communications may consist of:

■ encouraging a culture of comment and feedback;

■ formal review meetings with funders and suppliers;

■ making use of staff meetings or supervision events with individuals;

- holding public meetings;
- setting up sub-groups involving any of the above to look at specific issues.

From an information management perspective, ensuring that such communication takes place is essential, but it need not be time-consuming. Most of the options involve occasional events, which can be planned in advance. The communication needs to take place regularly, but it does not need to be constant.

Extending your horizons

Communication with your existing contacts alone is unlikely to be enough to ensure the effectiveness of your organisation. Interaction between groups of essentially similar people is easier than interaction with 'outsiders' but it is also less likely to lead to any fundamental challenge to existing ways of doing things or to innovation. Being creative, being able to respond to rapidly changing circumstances, is a requirement of success, if not survival, in a fast-changing environment.

So you also need to explore the exchange of information and ideas with people and sources who are not part of your current circle of regular contacts. This may cause a confusion of feelings. It may be fun to explore or you may resent the time it takes. You may be frightened of missing something important or your work may be rendered almost impossible by time spent wading through information to no apparent purpose.

There is no easy way to balance the demands of the tasks in hand with the time and space you need to look ahead and to be creative. How people develop new ideas is also a highly personal process. There are no absolute rules to it at all. It is, however, all too easy to explore a number of issues half-heartedly without benefiting from the process. There are a number of steps you can take, with more or less self-discipline, to give some organisation to the process.

Practical steps towards change

First, you can decide what proportion of your time should be spent on such exploration. This will depend very much on your analysis of your area of work and the rate at which it is or could be affected by change. One of the authors of this book now works solely around information issues, which is a subject of constant change. He spends about a third of his time on trying to see and assess what is new. Five years ago, in a different and more tried and tested line of work, the proportion was more like one-twentieth. The point is not the amount of time you decide to devote to looking ahead, but the fact that you have consciously allocated an appropriate and set amount of time to this process.

The next step is to realise that you cannot explore every potentially interesting new idea or every possible change to every aspect of your work. You have to select a few aspects you want to explore further – possibly to do with funding, possibly with how technology will affect your work, possibly with developments in 'good practice' in your area of work. It would generally be advisable to concentrate on topics which are giving you grounds either for real optimism or for real concern.

Example 20 Electronic networking

Katya is interested in how communities can use new technologies, so she subscribes to an electronic mailing list. She immediately starts to receive, on average, about fifty messages a week about all aspects of the topic – political, practical, technical, organisational. During a supervision session she mentions the volume of traffic and the time it takes to read all the messages.

Her line manager's first response is to suggest de-subscribing, because it is not a good use of her time. However, Katya has found some of the information very relevant and would be reluctant to lose it. Together they agree that Katya will define more clearly what she is interested in, and will only read the contributions that are relevant. She will delete all the rest without reading them or after the merest glance.

This works well. Katya manages to cut her reading down to five messages a week that are relevant. Often they put her in contact with other specialist practitioners which might otherwise take her months to find. The benefit is not just to her, but to the organisation.

Finally you should decide on appropriate means to pursue your chosen priorities, taking into account the amount of time that you have allocated to the process. Options include:

- collaborative work with others, where you keep up to date in one area and agree to share your information with a colleague, possibly in another organisation, who is keeping up to date on another topic (such as in Example 11);
- buying in expertise and opinion from people who are more closely involved in changes in the area in which you are interested;
- attending conferences;
- reading relevant publications;
- participating in professional organisations, informal networks or electronic discussion lists.

Some self-discipline is required with all of these, especially the latter two, if you are not going to start reading about or listening to information about all sorts of other subjects which are not on your list. For a manager, the key to success is to reach agreement with staff on which subject areas are to be explored, so as to ensure that all priority issues are investigated. The manager should both encourage creative exploration by staff and at the same time give it some direction and set clear limits.

Making information exchange mutually successful

All successful communication depends on understanding each other. That is why we have language. When it comes to communication between organisations the need is not simply for language but for an understanding of what each organisation wants from the relationship and how each organisation works.

Even in the most informal and casual of links created for the exchange of information between organisations, there are important questions:

- Why is my organisation making the link?
- Why are the other parties involved making the link? (It will be more sustainable if all parties are aware of why the others are involved and to what extent they are getting what they expected.)
- What sort of information (content, quality, timeliness) needs to be exchanged and why?
- Who is responsible for confidentiality and data protection policy?
- Is the level of commitment in terms of time and resources adequate for the purpose in hand and clear?
- Are the practical arrangements for the linkage appropriate to the responsibilities assigned to it and the amount of work involved.
- What are the procedures for breaking the link, should any party desire this.

The time and effort taken to work through these questions will vary. For more informal communication, such as that of an electronic mailing list, it would clearly be inappropriate to spend hours working out the rules. However, even in such cases, there are likely to be implicit assumptions among participants for what is or is not regarded as acceptable behaviour. One of these assumptions is the limit to which you are obliged to participate. Don't let others set your priorities. Just because someone sends you lots of information, you don't have to read it – especially if it is about their policies, which you cannot influence, or about parts of their work which don't affect you. Equally, if they ask you for information which takes a lot of time to produce, you can always offer them something slightly different which is already to hand.

In other situations, like direct practical collaboration in complex work, the need to be explicit is obvious. It may be that in those circumstances the amount of information exchanged is so detailed and complete that each organisation becomes dependent on the other not abusing their knowledge, for example in competing against each other for future contracts. Total protection against such abuse is not possible. However, written agreements or codes of conduct on confidentiality of information can make clear what is expected.

Problems are more likely to occur where the rules are unclear. The history of local partnerships involving both public-sector and community organisations offers examples where power relationships and institutional agendas have been ignored or hidden and where there has been a lack of clarity in the proposed linkages. Trust cannot be assumed. The questions of who is contributing information to the partnership, of what value and for what purpose, need to be asked. In situations of inequality or lack of trust, a gradual build-up of the amount and quality of information exchanged should be considered.

Making your communications accessible

Information is only of any use if the people you are communicating with can access it satisfactorily. It is the responsibility of the information provider to take this into account.

When you know the requirements of the particular person you are communicating with, you can adapt your materials to meet their particular needs. However, what works well for one person may not be much use to another, so when you are providing information to a broad audience you may have to make some compromises. Nevertheless, it is worth taking steps to ensure that your information is as accessible as possible.

Some of the simpler measures include:

- using clear type of a reasonably large size (the Royal National Institute for the Blind recommend 12-point minimum and can supply more detailed guidelines);
- choosing colours carefully so that they contrast properly;
- writing in plain English.

These principles should be applied to all information, regardless of who it is for. Even if someone is capable of understanding long, convoluted sentences in small type, printed in red on a black background, they will not thank you for making them do so. The content of the information is likely to get lost in the struggle to absorb it.

You may also want to offer your information in a variety of formats. There are several worth considering.

- **Large print** – once material is on computer, it is very little effort to set the type size larger and reprint.

- **Audio tape** – this can be time-consuming to prepare, but it is something that volunteers are often willing to undertake if you don't have access to a suitable service.
- **Braille** – this is not as expensive or as difficult as it used to be now that specialised programs are able to produce Braille more or less directly from a computer disk.
- **Documents on computer disk** – text-to-speech programs allow a computer to read out documents directly from a computer file. Provided that the recipient has a suitable program this is often the quickest and most useful way to provide your material.

Plentiful guidance on all these topics is readily available (see *Further Information*).

Don't forget, also, to consider whether your information needs to be translated into languages which your audience prefers.

Managing the boundaries: reception

Whatever you agree about how information will be exchanged, your organisation still has to deliver. Where you have nominated specific contact people they will be the main channel of communication. However, contact people aren't always available. Then there are all the people or organisations contacting you for the first time – which may turn into valuable partners in the future. Every phone call or other contact matters, and how an organisation deals with the minutiae of communication counts for as much as its strategic approach to the relationship.

The telephone and other reception channels

How do you feel when you phone up an organisation you are not very familiar with, only to find that the person you want to speak to isn't there? Does your reaction depend on how your call is treated? Of course it does. If you get a friendly voice, who is clear about when the person you need will be available, who offers to take a message, and who appears to grasp the main points of your message, you feel that the organisation is safe to deal with. Even better if the person answering the call manages to deal with the matter, or refers you to someone who can.

Far too many organisations give the opposite impression: the person you first speak to takes ages to answer the phone, resents your call, doesn't know anything helpful, and can't really be bothered to try helping you out. First impressions count, and a poor way of dealing with the outside world is often symptomatic of an organisation which doesn't take the management of information and communications seriously.

Your receptionist can be a key organisational resource – even if you don't have one. What matters is that the person taking calls and receiving visitors should be regarded as one of the information hubs of the organisation. If the task is rotated round a number of people, no matter. While they're on duty, the principles apply.

A good receptionist not only gives a good image, but also makes the flow of information round an organisation much smoother and more efficient. They can also save other staff an enormous amount of time.

The receptionist should:

- answer the telephone and greet visitors promptly, in a friendly, helpful and efficient way;
- have access to an accurate, up-to-date diary of *all* relevant staff in the organisation;
- know enough about the organisation to understand many of the messages left, and to be able to refer callers to other relevant people if appropriate;
- prompt the caller leaving a message, to ensure that the message is as useful as possible.

Answering the phone

It may be helpful to consider three prerequisites for the receptionist to be able to deal with callers promptly. First, they must have access to the phone, and be able to pick it up quickly. This doesn't mean that they have to be just sitting there waiting for the phone to ring, but it does mean that there are some jobs which do not go well with reception. Photocopying, for example, could take someone away from their desk, and they are bound to be right in the middle of a complex double-sided landscape run when a key contact rings up. Creative work is hard when you are likely to be interrupted frequently. However, the reception task may fit well with data-processing activities, such as entering membership records onto the computer, or scanning newspapers and magazines for relevant material and clipping or indexing it.

Secondly, the receptionist needs to be able to transfer calls to the right people quickly and accurately. Partly this is a matter of the right equipment; equally it is a matter of training. 'I think I remember how to transfer you ... ' followed by a lengthy silence, then 'Good morning, X organisation!' is not the model to follow.

Thirdly, training in telephone technique may also be appropriate. Without being artificially bright and cheerful, it is still possible to learn how to be positive and friendly – and also how to cope appropriately if the caller is unhappy and wants to complain or report a problem.

Access to the diary

It is not far fetched to claim that the efficiency of many organisations would be transformed if they maintained an accurate central diary of staff movements. Increasingly, the tools for this are available on computer; but traditional manual systems can be just as effective.

The key is that *no one* should be exempt: not the director, not the maverick outreach worker, not the two-days-a-week secondee who is developing a new project. This works only if it is taken seriously from the top down, so it is a management issue; it must become so much part of the organisation's culture that people do it automatically.

The director can then empower the receptionist to insist on knowing where people are going when they leave the building, and when they will be back, as well as expecting all their appointments to be entered into a diary which is accessible, whether or not they are in the building themselves. Anyone can still keep their own diary, of course, but only if it doesn't diverge from the official one.

The result of having a complete central diary is that anyone, inside the organisation or outside, needing to contact people or arrange a meeting knows when they can do so. In many cases the receptionist can make provisional bookings (or in some cases even firm ones) in people's absence – saving enormous time and effort, and repeated wasted calls.

There are also other management spin-offs, in being able to monitor how people use the time they spend out of the office and in being able to take prompt action if people become unreliable about being available when they said they would – which is often a symptom of other problems.

Knowing the organisation and the people

Reception work is often given to temporary or new staff. This is a bad idea. A good receptionist needs to be able to judge what a message means, how important it might be, and who to pass it on to if the right person isn't going to be available for some time. For this, there is often no substitute for experience (though good briefing obviously helps). This not only helps to ensure that the receptionist records the most important parts of the message accurately; it also means that the organisation as a whole is making the response, not just the individual the message was for.

Taking complete and accurate messages

All staff, not just the official receptionist, should be able to take messages well. The organisation should start by defining the minimum set of information to be recorded. This includes:

■ the date of the call;

- the time of the call;
- who the call was for;
- the name and (if any) the organisation of the person calling;
- the phone number on which the call can be returned;
- the times the person will be available on that number;
- the day and time by which they need to have been called back if there is a deadline;
- any message they wish to leave.

The person taking the call should prompt the caller, politely, for each of these pieces of information. If possible they should also give an indication of when the call is likely to be returned. This partly depends on the diary, partly on their knowledge of how busy the person is and how high up their priority list this call is likely to be.

In many organisations it may be worth producing telephone message slips with slots for all the information above, to ensure that nothing gets left out (and also so that people can identify phone messages among all the other pieces of paper on their desks). Whether or not this is done, proper guidance should be given to ensure that all staff are competent to take messages.

Handling enquiries

Although it is outside the scope of this book, it is worth noting that handling enquiries as part of your service is a different, and more specialised job from reception.

You should have staff (or volunteers) specially trained for this role, both in the content of the information or advice that they may be called on to give, and in the skills necessary to draw out from the caller the real nature of their enquiry and to deal with it sympathetically. Finally, you must have an adequate information system to back up the knowledge of those dealing with enquiries and a suitable recording system to provide information to managers and funders.

Pressure point

I'm worried about people who give out information to the public without checking their facts.

People have an enormous reluctance to admit that they don't know something, or to spend time looking it up. Quite often, they will give wrong information or claim not to have the information at all, rather than check – particularly if checking means actually looking it up instead of just shouting across the room to a colleague. The consequences for the organisation can be serious if information turns out to be wrong or incomplete: at best, people's image of the organisation will go down; at worst, clients may end up in real difficulties.

If your organisation depends on its reputation for giving sound information, or even if you just mind about your public image, it is important to tackle this firmly:

- formulate clear guidelines about how enquiries should be processed and how information should be checked before it is given out;
- ensure that all those who deal with the public are given adequate training, not just when they start off, but regularly;
- ensure that the resources where people are supposed to check their information can actually do the job: are they up to date, accurate and easy to use?

GETTING HELP

Even if we sometimes feel that we ought to, we cannot be expected to know the solution to every problem off the top of our heads. When we don't, there are a variety of options for trying to work out an appropriate response. These range from the most common, such as thinking about it or discussing it with a colleague, to seeking more formal assistance. This assistance could include formal management techniques or tools and the use of external expertise.

Management tools

Management involves collecting information, making decisions, monitoring and evaluation and taking new decisions as a result. There are a host of techniques or tools which managers can apply to these aspects of their job. Most involve the use of information. Indeed, a collective term for these techniques can be 'management information'.

However, when it comes to applying management tools to managing information itself – to take decisions, to monitor and evaluate the use of information – we find we are still in the early stages of development. There is not an established collection of tried and trusted techniques for this purpose. Below we outline some of the areas of managing information for which techniques can be learnt and applied. We do not go into detail here; many techniques can be found illustrated in *Information Management for Development Organisations* (see *Further information*). Look at the following outlines in the light of your own experience and see if they help you to develop ways of analysing or responding to situations.

Information audit

An information audit describes the process of identifying all the information resources in an organisation, what they consist of, who is responsible for them and their purpose. As a tool, an audit can have a value as an occasional exercise, used to get a clear idea of what you have. It can also be used as a component of understanding your organisation's information architecture, in which case it is worth creating a mechanism to try and keep it up to date.

The amount of time you dedicate to carrying out occasional information audits, or the level of detail you go into will vary. One example aimed at showing the main information flows affecting an organisation externally and internally is given below. Often such a general picture can be adequate to stimulate an informed discussion of what is working well and what isn't.

More detailed investigation can then be carried out over the areas where information flow is not felt to be satisfactory. It is worth stressing that what is being audited is use of information, not other commodities. Hence, in the example below, financial information is shown flowing between various stakeholders, whilst the actual flow of money is not.

Example 21 An information audit

Elaine is the manager of a community business-development unit, and she wants to check that the unit is managing its information efficiently. She starts by sketching out what she sees as the main information flows between the unit and the various external people and organisations with which it interacts (Figure 1). She also tries to include important exchanges of information which occur independently between some of these stakeholders.

She then tries to show how this information is handled by the people responsible for different tasks within the unit (Figure 2). For example, the development workers need to learn from the experiences of community businesses to improve their own practice. This information, however, is also needed by the person trying to lobby policy makers and develop a long-term strategy for the unit. Elaine herself needs some of this information in order to report to the management committee.

She circulates the sketches to all staff, explaining that they are her assessment of what should be happening. She asks people to think about whether the sketches reflect what is actually happening and whether people are getting the information they need at the right time, in the right format and the right degree of accuracy. She subsequently devotes the main part of a staff meeting to a follow-up discussion.

It is commented that the archive, kept by the administrative worker, is not that useful for the organisational development team because it is hard to extract 'lessons learnt' from files full of daily administrative and financial information. One person complains that he feels poorly informed about long-term plans for the unit because these seem to be discussed most in the pub after evening meetings which he can't get to. This in turn leads to a discussion of whether Figure 1 expresses

adequately the large level of informal exchange of information between external stakeholders.

The discussion therefore raised awareness of all these issues. It also led to further work on plotting information flows in the external environment, to aid the unit in ensuring that it is not bypassed by outside events and ideas.

Figure 1 - Information Flows and the External Environment

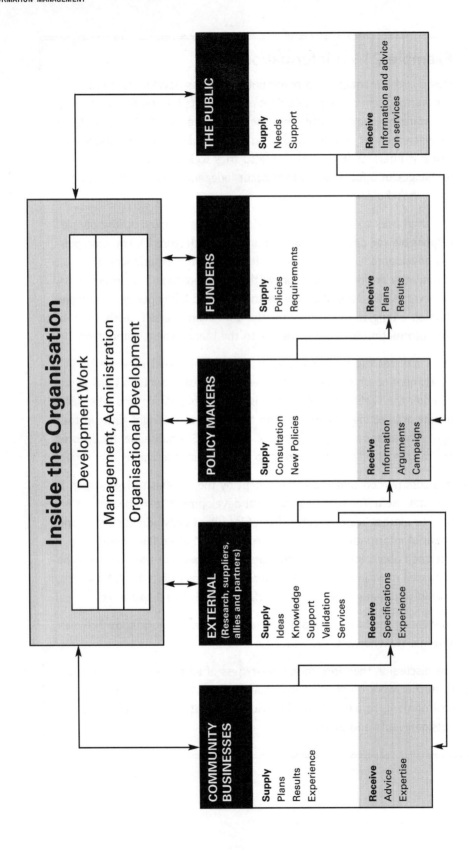

Figure 2 - Information Flows Inside the Organisation

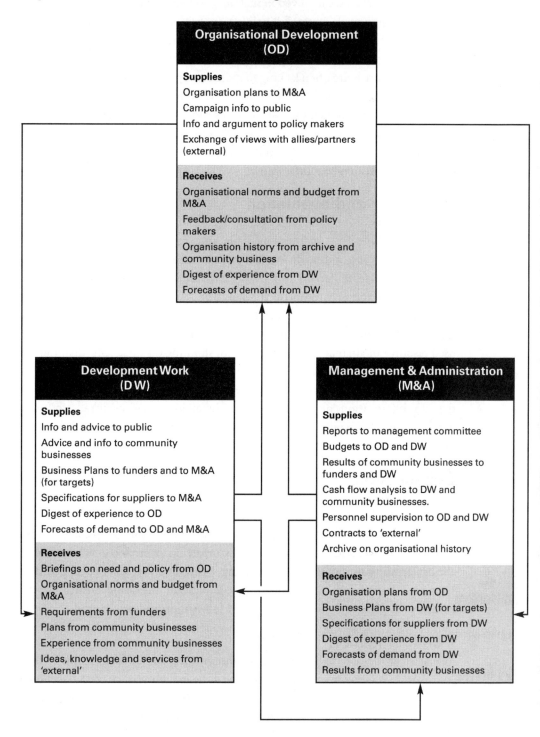

Choosing areas for investment

There are two processes involved in making good investment decisions. The first involves working up each possibility in a way that ensures that what is proposed is the best solution for the perceived need. An example of this applied to the choice of information technologies is given in Chapter 11. However, in the real world the resources are often lacking to meet every perceived need. You also need a process for choosing which of a number of good proposals is most deserving of investment. The main issues involved in this process are discussed in Chapter 4, under 'Information economics'. A detailed example of the use of a more formal method which can be used is given in *Information Management for Development Organisations* (see *Further information*).

Monitoring and evaluation

You need to be constantly monitoring the production, use and exchange of information by your organisation. This can be achieved in part through quantitative means, although these should be treated with caution. It is, for example, possible to record how often individual information resources are consulted; for expensive resources this may be advisable. However, knowing that a certain document has been consulted 50 times does not automatically mean that anyone found it useful. Nor do such measurements usually catch the most-used resource of all, that is colleagues within shouting distance. One quantitative measure which could be the information equivalent of 'reporting by exception' is to take a note of every item from every meeting which ends with the realisation that an information or communication breakdown has occurred. In most organisations this would soon be a long list capable of offering real food for thought.

Consultation

Your colleagues or staff are your best source of understanding how well information is being managed. Ask them regularly what they need, whether they are receiving it, whether it is useful and what they think other people need. More detailed reflection and discussion, possibly involving external contacts, can offer the opportunity to move from monitoring – checking that what is supposed to happen is happening – to evaluation – looking at the value created by the processes in place and seeing if they need to be improved or changed.

Communication

You need to be able to record and communicate your understanding of how information is being managed. This can be done in a number of ways depending on what is being described and who needs to understand it. Drawings are often used to show information resources and the arrangements and flows between them. You may wish to experiment with shapes or ways of grouping points in order to find a style which you think expresses the information you are concerned with. A growing number of software tools are also available. Whatever you do, you should be aware that for some people even the best diagram is a meaningless scribble. You may also find the following rules, based loosely on those given to students of 'systems' on an Open University course, may be helpful in making the process useful.

- Do not confuse any informal mapping you undertake with the standardised forms which exist for certain professional purposes. If you are using a formal method, say so and stick to it. If not, then be aware that this is not an exact science. It is a skill which you will develop with practice and through seeing what forms make best sense to you or your colleagues.
- Be clear in your own mind about the purpose of the diagram you are developing. Experiment a little to see what form of diagram is going to help you achieve your purpose.
- Diagrams can be used to clarify your own thinking.
- If using the diagram to communicate with others, make sure it is clear. Too much detail or too much inter-connection of different parts can make it hard to understand.
- One way of achieving both clarity and detail is to summarise detail under a single term on one diagram and then produce another diagram to show the detail of the 'sub-system'.
- Diagrams need not be entirely self-explanatory. Headings or text may be used to help explain them. If you are using different types of line, arrow, box or colour to give specific meaning it is helpful to explain this clearly to the reader, but overuse of such symbols may make the diagram difficult to follow. Think also of what will photocopy well and what, such as colour, will disappear in the process.
- Use what space you have. A cramped diagram is always hard to follow.

Employing professional information workers

Because we all use information all the time, everyone needs to have a certain level of competence in handling it effectively. However, it is always worth considering whether professional help would be useful as well.

One option for organisations is to employ professional information workers on the staff. This is especially likely to be the case where information provision to outside users is one of the main purposes of the organisation. Professional staff will know how to find the information you need, classify and store it efficiently, and present it to users in accessible ways. Their tasks might include:

- maintaining and exploiting an organisation's archive;
- producing bulletins, journals or magazines;
- running a telephone enquiry line;
- management of a Web site;

- producing information sheets;
- enabling telephone or personal callers to research their own information in a library or on computer databases.

In a larger organisation where staff need a lot of information in order to do their work, a professional librarian or other information worker may be required to manage your organisation's internal information. This could include:

- operating a library;
- devising classification schemes;
- preparing current awareness bulletins;
- running a loan service for books or reports;
- helping staff to carry out research on the Internet;
- clipping and filing newspaper and magazine articles;
- keeping abreast of current legislation;
- preparing reading lists organised by subject area;
- providing access for other staff members to information held on computer databases, and helping them to use them effectively;
- generally taking a proactive approach to assessing people's information needs, instead of just waiting for people to come looking for information.

The Further information section includes additional resources on employing professional information staff.

Employing consultants

If the amount of information work your organisation needs doesn't warrant the employment of permanent staff, you may still benefit from professional input from time to time. The types of work where it may make sense to use a consultant include:

- working out a classification system;
- setting up a Web site;
- reviewing your information strategy;
- carrying out an information audit;
- reviewing policies on confidentiality, data protection, and other technical areas of information management;
- carrying out independent research among your staff or users;
- training staff members in information skills.

There may also be jobs from time to time where you need extra help. For example, when an organisation moves offices there is often a massive one-off archiving blitz. It may well be worth bringing in someone with professional skills to help with this.

The key to getting the best out of an information consultant, as with any consultant, is to know what you want. Either in the initial brief, or as the first part of the work, you need to spell out what your aims are and what kind of input you are expecting from the consultant. You should also consider the following points.

- Always take up references before employing a consultant.
- When you take up references be sure to ask not just about the consultant's technical competence but also about how good they are at sticking to deadlines and relating to the people they are working with.
- Except for very small amounts of work, where a simple exchange of letters may well be sufficient, set out the expectations of both sides in a written contract.
- Get your internal procedures right, so that the consultant has a contact who can provide a quick and authoritative response to any points the consultant might raise.
- If you employ more than one consultant in related areas, make absolutely sure that you have put in place a mechanism for enabling them to co-operate and for sorting out any disagreements that might arise between them.
- Ensure that issues such as copyright on any materials produced are clarified in writing.
- Don't expect the consultant to do all the work. They may be able to set up a beautiful system, but if you have not participated in developing it, the likelihood is that you won't know enough about how it works to be able to maintain it in good order.

Good consultants are rarely cheap. Before employing a consultant make sure that you define their task so that what they do brings genuine benefit to the organisation. Above all, you want their work to help you make decisions; they will have to spend time getting to know the organisation, but a long report which describes the organisation in detail is unlikely to tell you much that you don't already know, and is unlikely to be read much. Apply the principles of this book: what you are usually looking for is a much briefer report spelling out the key background points (the 'headlines') and with the detail reserved for the recommendations. You can always get the consultant to come back and explain where the ideas came from if necessary. You should also beware of a consultant who produces recommendations without trying out their ideas on you first, either verbally or in an interim report. Only in that way can you and the consultant both be confident that the recommendations have a chance of working.

Help with IT

Many important developments have come about because new possibilities offered by IT just take off, rather than as a result of deliberate planning. For example, the growing use of e-mail has sometimes happened more because the technology is available, than because people had thought through how they wanted to use it.

Managers with no detailed knowledge of IT have to find out from somewhere what the options are, but without being pushed by the technical people into spending money the organisation can't afford on inappropriate developments.

Good decision-making therefore depends on an effective partnership between managers and technical people. This may require some changing of attitudes on both sides. Managers have to take on responsibility for IT issues and be prepared to take advice from technical specialists. IT specialists must be prepared to work with managers, to accommodate organisational issues and to talk to managers in their own terms without taking refuge in technical jargon.

What your 'expert' ought to be able to tell you is:

- what you should expect a good product in this area of technology to be capable of;
- what are the foreseeable trends for the next few years;
- how this development could contribute to the agency's overall aims;
- what kind of costs are involved;
- what timescale and input of staff time would be realistically required;
- both the pros and the cons, the risks and benefits, of any proposal – and the potential risks of *not* doing something.

The manager has to ask key questions, and know which questions to ask – the list above is a good starting point – in order to get advice which will contribute sensibly to the strategic policy decisions which have to be made. If you are in this position you should not be satisfied until you are sure you have understood what you are being told.

chapter ⑩

STAYING LEGAL

The best single detailed resource on all legal matters affecting voluntary organisations is *The Voluntary Sector Legal Handbook* (see *Further information*). See also specific publications, such as *Data Protection in Voluntary Organisations*.

Data protection

The 1998 Data Protection Act – in force from 1 March 2000 – applies to virtually all organisations. Unlike the previous (1984) Act, it extends data protection to manual, paper-based filing systems, and to some photographic, audio and video records. It also incorporates into law much of what has previously been merely good practice.

The Act applies to 'personal data' – information about identifiable living individuals, which could include staff, volunteers, clients, donors, members, and people the organisation might lobby or invite to its events.

The heart of the Act is the eight Data Protection Principles. These are, in essence, that:

1 personal data must be processed fairly and lawfully;
2 personal data must be obtained only for specified purposes, and then must not be used for anything else;
3 personal data must be adequate, relevant and not excessive;
4 personal data must be accurate and, where necessary, kept up to date;
5 personal data must not be kept longer than necessary;
6 personal data must be processed in accordance with the rights of data subjects;
7 appropriate technical and organisational security measures must be taken;
8 personal data may only be transferred outside western Europe (or put on the Internet) if certain conditions are met.

'Fair processing' (Principle 1) includes the provision that data subjects must know who is processing their data and what for. It also specifies that in some cases you must get the data subject's consent to process their data. Consent is nearly always required in the case of 'sensitive' data – information about a person's racial or ethnic origin, beliefs, politics, health, sex life and criminal record.

Data subjects' rights include being able to find out if you are processing data about them, and to see a copy of what you hold. Data subjects also have the right to prevent you using their information for direct marketing (which includes writing to them or phoning them up to ask for donations to a charity).

The Act is complex, with numerous exemptions and qualifications. In some cases it will be important to take advantage of these (for example where it is a case of balancing conflicting rights and interests between two different people). In the main, however, a few simple guidelines will ensure that you don't go far wrong.

- Ensure that anyone you hold information about knows that you hold it, what you use it for, and who you might pass it on to. Often a short statement on your forms and leaflets is all that you will need.
- Get consent for holding people's information wherever possible, and get explicit consent, in writing if possible, for any 'sensitive' information you want to hold.
- Make sure that you offer people the chance to opt out of any direct marketing.
- Design your systems so that you can easily comply with any request by a data subject to see the records you hold on them.
- Make appropriate security arrangements, both for manual and for computer systems, depending on how sensitive the information is. For example, do you need to restrict access to rooms or filing cabinets? Do you need passwords on your computer systems? Do you back up files regularly so that you don't lose vital information?
- Train or brief your staff in what they are allowed to do with people's information, what they are not allowed to do, and whom they have to ask if they are unsure.
- Check whether you need to 'notify' the Data Protection Commissioner about your data-processing activities. (This applies only to computer-based, not manual systems.)
- Appoint a member of staff as data protection compliance officer, so that they know it is part of their job to find out about data protection in more detail and to keep the organisation within the law.

Copyright

The law on copyright can be complex. Some things that people assume they are permitted to do, because it happens frequently, may actually be a breach of the law. The key points are:

- Copyright in material which employees create in the course of their employment belongs to the employer, unless there is an agreement to the contrary.

- It is important to clarify the copyright position regarding any materials (including, for example, a Web site) created by non-employees – volunteers as well as external workers. The simplest way to do this is by a sentence in the contract or letter commissioning the work.
- Copyright exists, it does not have to be claimed – unlike some other intellectual property rights – and the © symbol is not obligatory in the UK. It is conventional to indicate on publications who owns the copyright and the date of first publication (to help users know whether copyright has expired).
- It is important to ensure that an organisation either owns, or has assigned to it, copyright in reports, brochures, photographs, or any other material it may wish to publish.
- Generally you need permission (often referred to as a licence) to copy or publish someone else's copyright material. This includes reproducing articles or newspaper cuttings as part of an information service, even just for internal use. Charities can normally get a free licence for this purpose from the Newspaper Licensing Agency.
- You do not need permission to extract the information itself from a copyright work and re-use it, provided you put it into your own words.
- There is provision for 'fair dealing', when individual researchers can copy information for their own purposes, as long as it is only a small proportion of the work. Many publicly accessible libraries can give guidance on this.

Defamation

In brief, libel is a defamatory statement which is published in any permanent form. (A verbal defamatory comment is slander.) 'Published' means that the statement must be made to a third party. To be defamatory, the statement must refer to an identifiable living person or a corporate body, and must 'tend to lower [that person] in the estimation of... society'.

Since 'publishing' a defamation requires the comment to be made to only one other person, a private letter can be just as defamatory as a leaflet or magazine article which is distributed to thousands of people.

It is worth developing an organisational culture of not 'slagging off' other people or organisations, both on principle and to reduce the risk of the organisation becoming implicated in a defamation. There are defences, and defamation insurance is available, but the best defence is not to let the situation arise in the first place.

Acceptable-Use Policies for e-mail

Many organisations now find that they need to clarify how staff may use e-mail facilities provided by the employer. Generally an Acceptable-Use Policy will cover two broad areas:

- how much of the employer's resources may legitimately be used for private activities;
- what types of content are to be avoided.

Just as most organisations tacitly allow a certain amount of private use of the office phone, so most tolerate a certain amount of e-mail usage (and private Web surfing). Some, however, ban it completely and many monitor the staff's Web activity and outgoing e-mail messages. If private use is not banned outright, it is worth indicating what level of use might be considered acceptable. (In one celebrated case, an IT manager was dismissed for grossly over-using the Internet from work for booking a holiday. The dismissal was held to be fair.)

There may also be a good case for limiting the size of private files people may transmit. While a ten-line message will not over-stretch the organisation's resources, a series of large picture files may well start to affect the availability of the system for other users. There are technical means of enforcing such a limit if you suspect that users are not respecting it.

There appears to be a tendency for people to treat e-mails less seriously than other written communication. For this reason it is worth reminding staff that: (a) because e-mail is stored on so many successive computers during its transmission they should assume that there is a permanent record of it somewhere in the system, even if they think they have deleted it; and (b) certain types of material are inappropriate. Inappropriate uses or materials typically include:

- harassment of any kind, whether directed at a specific individual or broadcast more generally;
- racist, sexist, homophobic or other discriminatory materials;
- pornography, risqué jokes and indecent images;
- defamatory statements.

You should also remind users to think carefully about what they put into e-mails. The organisation is just as bound by commitments made in an e-mail as by written or verbal statements. There have been examples of organisations inadvertently entering into expensive unwanted contracts because a staff member made a commitment in an e-mail, without the content being authorised or checked.

Retention policy

The question of when and how you archive or throw away material has been discussed in Chapter 6. There are a few legal aspects to this.

- Some material has by law to be kept indefinitely (e.g. key documents relating to a limited company), or for a specified minimum period (e.g. accounts, tax and other financial records).

- In other cases you may be guided from outside. For example, a company providing professional indemnity insurance will undoubtedly want you to keep case records for as long as any liability might arise.
- The Data Protection Act stipulates that information must not be kept longer than necessary. In the first instance it is up to you to judge what is necessary, depending on the purpose for which the information is held.

If in doubt, consult an expert such as your solicitor or accountant.

USING COMPUTERS EFFECTIVELY

Managing IT

By far the most important consideration in using IT well is to start by knowing what you are trying to do, and to design your processes and procedures well. After that, getting the technology to serve your needs is a much easier proposition. This section covers a few basic principles which all organisations ought to consider.

The management committee must take the major decisions. It can take as much technical advice as it likes, but in the end the issues are not technical; they are to do with what the organisation is trying to achieve, and how it is going to get there.

There must be a staff member with responsibility for IT. Most users do not want to be technical experts, or to worry about how well the computer is performing. However, somebody has to do this. It often makes most sense to give one person the main responsibility for ensuring that your computer systems work effectively. As a rule of thumb, you could expect to need one full-time IT support person for 50 staff members. If you have a staff of 10 therefore, it would be reasonable to expect to allocate one day a week to this task.

The job description for an IT manager or IT support worker could include:

- acting as systems manager for your network (if you have one);
- providing IT support to computer users within the office (including inducting new staff);
- initial trouble-shooting of IT problems, and resolving them wherever possible;
- ensuring that data is routinely backed up;
- ensuring that all staff are able to organise their computer files in an effective way whether they are shared or for individual use;

- managing the distribution of documents in electronic format and of standard layouts and templates for documents;
- ensuring that software licences are adhered to;
- over-seeing computer security and anti-virus precautions;
- acting as data protection officer (although under the 1998 Act this is no longer exclusively an IT issue);
- keeping an inventory of all computer equipment, keeping maintenance records, and ensuring adequate maintenance provision;
- identifying bottlenecks and problems, making recommendations to solve them, keeping standard software and hardware recommendations under review, and providing input into future IT strategy.

You need to have a clear idea of when it is appropriate to bring in outside support. Few organisations have the resources to cover all their IT support needs in-house. You cannot, however, contract-out everything. Some problems or routine operations are too simple, too frequent, or too urgent for that. You need to find a balance, where in-house staff deal with basic day-to-day issues but know that they can call on external specialists for more complex problems.

Standardise the software that is used within your organisation as much as possible. This means, for example, that you should decide which version of a word-processing system you will use, and have this software set up in an identical – or very similar way – on all machines.

Important benefits of software standardisation

- Knowledgeable staff can help each other more easily if they are working on the same packages. It becomes worthwhile to train in-house 'experts' to a level where they can help others, without the expense of bringing in people from outside all the time.
- Staff who move from one part of the organisation to another, permanently or temporarily, do not have to be retrained.
- Training courses can be uniform across the organisation (and therefore cheaper and/or more frequent).
- It is easier to support, maintain and upgrade software if it is limited to a set number of packages.

- Information can more easily be exchanged between users of different computers.
- Standard procedures can be adopted throughout the organisation.
- Model and standard documents can be developed for use throughout the organisation.

If you standardise on software which is widely used in the outside world, it will make sharing information easier and reduce training needs of new staff. Many organisations have standardised on Microsoft Office for this reason.

When you have to use less standard software – for example if you need something specialised like a geographical information system – make sure that it can exchange information efficiently with standard packages (although be aware that data exchange between packages which involves changing formats is rarely perfect, and should be avoided if there is an obvious alternative).

Financing IT

Budget to replace your IT regularly. Although your older PCs will go on working for many years, they will be overtaken by software upgrades and your rising expectations. A good basis is to work to a four-year life for your hardware, if possible. This means budgeting to replace a quarter of your existing equipment each year, *in addition* to any new acquisitions.

Make clear provision for IT in the budget. As organisations become more dependent on IT, an *ad hoc* approach won't do. IT is just as important a part of the agency's financing as rent, salaries and the photocopier.

The management committee should consider where funding for IT will normally come from. Will it be a part of every funding application? Can you build it into core costs? Or will specific IT developments be funded as one-off projects in their own right? Will developments which save money in the long run have any sort of priority?

Training

You need a training policy. While computer hardware and software is still becoming relatively cheaper, the same is not true of staff time. It therefore makes enormous sense to ensure that staff not only have the most appropriate systems to help them achieve their tasks, but also the skills to use those systems effectively.

However, this is not just a matter of sending people on training courses when you – or they – feel like it. There is no alternative to working out properly what skills they need and then providing appropriate training, whether in-house, on an external course, or through individual coaching. Don't forget, also, that having time for training, and having the opportunity to practise immediately after a training course are vital if training is to be a success.

Making decisions about IT

Decisions about IT must be taken at the right level. In some cases this means the board or management committee. A large IT investment could easily change the way an organisation works just as much as a major reorganisation or a significant new piece of work. Decisions like this must be made at the top, regardless of whether the members feel technically competent. If necessary they should take advice.

Routine decisions, and work on the details of any development, should then normally be taken by staff. It is important, however, that decisions are taken within the framework of the organisation's policies and overall goals.

Finally, there is a level of day-to-day management of IT, as in the sample job description shown in the box above. Even here, it is essential that the person doing this work should not be given *carte blanche*; they should be given clear targets and guidelines, drawn from the policies.

Which decisions are appropriate for delegation may vary from organisation to organisation. The size of the organisation might be a factor; so might the experience of the managers or the time they have available. What is important is the need for *clarity* about which decisions can be taken at which level.

Example 22 How a clear policy can help staff make decisions

As an office manager, Charlotte is responsible for IT maintenance. Her agency has a policy of replacing its computers every four years. When an elderly computer breaks down, she therefore has a clear framework for deciding whether it is worth getting it fixed. It may be more cost-effective to bring forward the purchase of a new computer by a few months.

Implementing changes

Whoever has responsibility for taking the decisions should realise that unless they involve potential users in thinking through what would make their work easier or more effective, then even decisions made with the best of intentions are likely to end in failure. The overwhelming majority of UK investment in information technology fails to achieve its goals for this very reason.

Change is always stressful, in any organisation and in any setting; when you add in IT, with all its potential for technophobia and technical jargon, the problems are much greater. So even after you have decided what to do, you still have to make sure that you implement the changes or new systems properly. This means that you *must* plan any change properly.

- Find out from users, if you don't already monitor this, the shortcomings of current systems and ideas for what would work better.
- Work out what you want to do, taking account of feedback on the existing situation as well as your future goals.
- Inform or consult the users (again) as appropriate.
- Take account of their response. (Even if it is antagonistic, you need to work out how you are going to overcome the resistance.)
- Ensure that you allow enough time to introduce the change *and* deal with the inevitable problems and delays – wrong cables, lack of hard-disk space, missing printer drivers or whatever.
- Ensure that after you have got the computer system working again the users are given enough time to learn about the changes, and that their managers accept the fact that to start with they will inevitably be less productive.
- Build in training almost immediately after the change (so that people can practise on the new system but not get frustrated).

From the technical point of view, it is often wise to implement changes one step at a time. That way, if something doesn't work, you have a good idea of what is causing the problem. Change three things at once and you have a much harder job to find out whether one specific change is the problem or, indeed, whether it is the interaction between two of the changes.

The decision-making process: case study

The more complex the decision, the more elaborate the decision-making process may have to be, but the principles are always the same. Even an apparently 'technical' decision may have significant non-technical ramifications and therefore needs to be taken in its full context. For example, if a new e-mail system will involve training all the staff, how will this be done, and when? How much will it cost and where will the money come from?

There is no foolproof way to avoid the effects of 'creeping change' – where a series of small, apparently unconnected decisions end up having a major unforeseen effect. However, by ensuring that every decision is made carefully, and in its proper context, the risk of facing a nasty surprise in the future is minimised.

It is helpful to break the decision-making process down into stages, such as the seven stages outlined below. The case study here is deliberately straightforward, to illustrate the process, but the same steps would be followed for a major IT strategy review.

1 Clarify your objectives

It is very important that you start with your focus on the problem and its wider context, not on possible technical solutions. Put computers firmly at the back of your mind, and describe your objectives in terms of your overall goals – for the organisation overall if it is a big review, or for this particular development if it is a smaller decision. This has two benefits. Firstly, it ensures that everyone concerned can be involved, not just those who understand, or are keen on, technology. Secondly, it means that you don't automatically exclude non-IT solutions – perhaps a different way of working would be just as effective.

You must always be careful not to let technology take over. Everyone can see that it is rarely worth spending hours over a word processed memo, with fancy layout and clever graphics. Often a hand-written note is perfectly acceptable and quicker to produce. With complex IT systems, it is sometimes harder to make the judgement. Will the database really make such a difference that it's worth the investment? Do we really need a network in our three-person sub-office? Unless you are very clear about your aims, the temptation is just to get the technology because it's there and because everyone else is using it. They are not necessarily right.

Example 23 Andy's decision-making process

Andy is the service manager for a national organisation with six regional offices. He is concerned that the regional staff do not always use the most up-to-date versions of procedures, so he proposes an 'intranet', the objective of which would be 'to make current versions of all policies produced centrally available to all in the organisation'. When he proposes this to the chief executive, he is told to take a step back. The objectives could be stated as 'for all parts of the organisation to use the same procedures' and 'for new procedures to be introduced across the organisation as quickly and reliably as possible'. Now he can go on to think about how this might be achieved.

This example is continued in three further boxes in this section.

---

2 Decide criteria for choosing between different approaches

You will best be able to choose between different approaches to achieving your objectives if you work out key criteria to base the choice on.

These criteria should be phrased in as non-technical a way as possible. 'Every case worker should be able to get to up-to-date client details when they need them' is better than 'The client database should be multi-user with a response time of under 10 seconds'.

Since it is your managers who will need the answers, they must be able to understand both the questions and the answers. Many of the questions will be very specific to your organisation, and a solution which works in one organisation will not necessarily be suitable for another.

Example 23 (continued)

Andy decides on three key criteria.

- The system must be easy to use, even for staff with little computer confidence.
- The system must take as little administrative effort as possible, either at the national office or in the regional offices.
- Standard forms should look the same throughout the organisation.

---

3 Shortlist possibilities worth further investigation

In many ways this is the hardest step of all: it needs sufficient technical knowledge to know what is possible, combined with the imagination to see how each possibility might fit into a given organisation. Frequently, this is the point at which the agency needs to take outside advice.

It is a mistake to get too focused on specific hardware or software products. The answer to your needs might be a different way of using your existing system, or sending people for training, or paying someone to set things up in a different way, or even not using the computer at all, but changing your procedures in other ways. Being creative and thinking laterally at this point might give you a surprisingly different solution.

Be aware of the dangers of perfectionism, too. You need to consider in detail only those options which have a realistic chance of being adopted. If one or two software products are clear market-leaders, for example, there is no point researching all the others just in case.

Example 23 (continued)

Andy comes up with three options.

1 To set up the intranet.
2 To keep the existing system, but also: to bring in new procedures only at quarterly meetings of the regional staff; to give staff members strict instructions about using only the correct procedures and forms; and to monitor their use of procedures more closely.
3 To send out the procedures and forms on floppy disk, so that staff can print out their own copies as they need them.

---

4 Analyse the costs, benefits and risks for each option

In many cases, working out the costs is easy: you will be buying a product or paying for services. But don't forget to include other true costs, such as staff and management time. Benefits are harder to quantify, and it's quite unusual for them all to be economically measurable. If you improve your accounts package, you might be able to save on your audit fee, but how can you put a money value on being able to produce funding applications which are supported by better statistics, or on information for your clients which is more comprehensive?

Looking at the risks is something that few people do, but which is very worthwhile. A small change to your systems, with relatively small benefits, might be easier to introduce than a big change. All change is risky: people might be unsettled or rebel against it. In some cases it might be catastrophic if it goes wrong – if you give clients the wrong advice or lose accounting information, for example. Before making a choice it is, again, the management which has to decide whether the risks of any particular course of action are acceptable.

5 Consider possible 'knock-on' effects, positive or negative

You may have viewed many of the likely effects of the shortlist of possible changes as costs, benefits or risks, but you do need to check finally that you have considered all the knock-on effects. Will anyone's job description have to change? Will there be a period of disruption while you introduce the new system? Will you need new budget headings or new stationery? Will you have to rearrange the office layout? Only if you think about these questions in advance will you be able to plan how to minimise the bad effects and gain maximum advantage from the good ones.

6 Carry out any technical evaluations necessary

By this stage you might already know very precisely what your options are, or there may be some questions still to answer. You may have to choose between similar but competing products, or between suppliers who offer slightly different deals. At this point, again, you may need to take expert advice, to make sure that what you are about to buy does actually meet the requirements you set out at stage 1.

7 Make a final decision at the appropriate level

Stages 1 to 3 could well be quite quick – maybe as little as half a day, even for quite a major decision. Stages 4 to 6 may take a bit longer, but as you work through them you should find your options narrowing down, especially if you consult the relevant people as you go along. For example, at stage 4 your management may decide that some risks are unacceptably large, even if the potential benefits are great, or there may be an absolute ceiling on the budget which rules out some options on cost grounds.

But whether you are left with just one firm proposal or a number of options, you should have a formal decision-making point at the end. At this point, you should make a clear decision on what to do – whether it's to spend money, do something else, or do nothing – and you should also review the process by which you have got to that point, to make sure that all the stages have been explored adequately. The old carpentry adage 'measure twice, cut once' applies to more modern areas as well!

Example 23 (concluded)

After making his investigations and consulting staff, Andy decides that there are pros and cons to each option. He decides to recommend that, for holding policies and forms alone, the cost of an intranet cannot be justified, but that they should continue to consider it in the medium term as it would have other uses as well. Meanwhile he is going to exercise his management authority a bit more and see what difference he can make – taking the cheapest option of all.

Setting up a database

Many people automatically associate information on computer with databases. There is no question that computers do allow us to handle vast quantities of information in a systematic way, and to use the same information in many different ways for much less effort. A membership database can track who has paid their fees, produce mailing labels for the newsletter, generate lists of members by region, and so on, all of which would take much longer and probably be less accurate by hand.

Much has been written about database projects that went wrong – particularly large, spectacular disasters in commercial or government organisations. Yet disasters still happen. There is not space here to go into full detail, but a number of guiding principles are worth bearing in mind whenever the word 'database' comes up.

- **Be clear what you are trying to do**. Why are you developing the database? If it is to speed up a manual task, be clear how you expect it to do that, then check that it does before deploying it. If it is to consolidate information that is scattered all around the organisation into one consistent place, work out how you are going to prise the information from the people who currently have it and then make it worth their while to use the central database.

- **Start with the outputs**. Too many people begin a database project by trying to decide what information the database should hold. They end up with a system that they can put information into, but they can't get it out in the way they would find most useful. The best starting point is the lists, the sets of labels, the standard letters, the information on screen that you expect to use. Then work out how to set up the system to produce that.

- **Don't be too ambitious**. One of the commonest reasons for a database to fail is when it tries to stretch the available budget, or the available technology, or the skill of the developer, too far.

- **Be clear about who the project is for**. Whose needs are you trying to meet? That person, or group, has to be the one that decides whether a feature can be left out, and what types of process the database should support. You cannot develop a database for other people without involving them in the process, unless you are in a position afterwards to insist on them using the system your way.

- **Allow for new uses**. Your needs are bound to change over time. If databases are well designed then it is technically much easier to make changes, either to combine information from different sources or to develop an existing system. 'Not being too ambitious' need not, therefore, prohibit more elaborate databases in the future.

- **Use a professional**. Today's database tools are really too complex to be successfully used by self-trained amateurs. Money spent on a professional is well worth it in the long run, especially if you want to do new things with your data in the future.

■ **Allow twice as much money and twice as much time as you think reasonable** – even after you have been generous with your budgeting. Most database projects over-run their budget or their schedule or both, so you might as well accept this.

Using the Internet for e-mail

Most people find that, after some initial hesitation, e-mail becomes an essential part of their working lives. The technical requirements for a single user to have e-mail are not difficult to meet, especially now that most computers can be supplied with a modem ready-fitted, and there are many free Internet accounts available. Almost the only other issue is which phone line to plug the modem into. Since most e-mail transactions are short, there is usually no problem sharing a line with the user's telephone.

From the manager's point of view, the main concerns arise when more than one person at one site needs access to e-mail. To start with, many organisations just have one e-mail access point. Incoming messages may get printed off and given to people on paper. For replying, or sending outgoing messages, the user may have to wait for access to the specific computer with the e-mail facility. This loses much of the benefit of e-mail's immediacy. However, it is rarely worthwhile for each user to have a modem on their computer, each plugged into a phone line. Going through the switchboard may not be an option for technical reasons, and separate direct phone lines for each user, just for e-mail, are clearly not worth it financially. The other disadvantage of a single access point is that users cannot send internal e-mail to each other.

The solution is to run your e-mail over the network – assuming you have one. Everyone then uses a single modem or similar, attached to one machine on the network. This is slightly more complicated, and should be set up by a professional. The benefits are considerable. Each user can have their own e-mail address, so that messages go directly to them, without having to be passed through someone else. Internal e-mail is more valuable than it might appear, as it is a good way for exchanging documents electronically, or passing messages between people who are in the office at different times.

If you don't have a network, but do need e-mail, the single access point is likely to be the best compromise.

The choice of e-mail account (the facility you get from a Service Provider) can often appear daunting: there are so many Service Providers, all vying for your business. Most of the original 'free' accounts were aimed at home users. Now, however, the practice is spreading; accounts aimed at businesses and even specifically at charities and voluntary organisations are now coming along. The alternative is generally a standard dial-up account which could be all that is required by a small organisation.

Business accounts tend to be considerably more expensive, but include additional levels of support, and features such as 'domain name hosting'.

A domain name is well worth considering: for a fee, instead of your e-mail address being something like person@organisation.serviceprovider.net, it would be person@organisation.org.uk – which has several advantages. It makes your address easier to remember; it shows that you are beyond the most basic level of Internet use; and it means that if you change service provider in future your e-mail address doesn't have to change.

Despite all these technical considerations, for most organisations nowadays the decision on e-mail is as clear-cut as whether you need a word-processor: yes.

Setting up a Web site

With half the world telling you that no organisation can survive nowadays without a Web site, it's tempting just to cave in and agree to one being set up. This would be a mistake. Web sites can have a number of possible benefits, but the best way to approach them is to think of the Web as akin to publishing. An information-based site is something like a magazine. An 'intranet' – a site just for use within an organisation – is like an internal newsletter. A sales site has parallels with a mail-order catalogue.

Definitions

Many people use the words 'Internet' and 'Web' interchangeably. Here, however, they are used more precisely.

- The **Internet** is the infrastructure, the network of computers to which you can link your own computer, and which allows you to use a number of different services, including e-mail.
- The (World Wide) **Web** is one type of content available over the Internet: publicly accessible pages of information, containing text and images, with a strong design element. The 'address' of a Web page usually starts http://www. (or just www).

However, these analogies must not be taken too far. The Web is much more interactive than a paper-based magazine. Readers can just click a mouse to follow links from one page to another, even if the pages are on opposite sides of the world. They can be invited to respond and make direct contact by e-mail. On a growing number of sites they can not only view products, but go on to place orders and pay by credit card.

However, where the comparison is valid is that setting up a Web site is just as big an undertaking as deciding to launch a new magazine, newsletter or catalogue. Key questions should be considered fully before you start.

- **What are we trying to achieve?** Just as with any other project, you will get far more benefit, and make far better decisions, if you know what you are trying to achieve before you start.

- **Who is our audience?** You must design any publication with the audience in mind. The Web is no exception. This leads on to the next two questions.

- **What does our audience want from the site?** If you decide that your 'readers' need specific information, the design of the site has to make it easy for them to get it.

- **Does our audience have Web access?** Although access is spreading very quickly, you still need to check that you can actually reach the people you want to. In particular, workers in other voluntary organisations may well have access at home but not at the office, and they may be reluctant to use the Web for work activities when they are off duty.

- **Is our Web site fully accessible?** Bear in mind that people may have obsolete computers or software, slow modems, or disabilities which make a fancy site hard to use. Check all aspects of the accessibility of your site.

- **Is our site well designed?** Almost anyone with a computer can create a Web site, but it takes a good designer to make it easy to use, attractive to look at, technically reliable, and consistent with your other publications and your house style.

- **Can we keep the site up to date?** Unless the site is expressly designed as an archive (perhaps of material published elsewhere on paper), users will expect it to change frequently and be kept up to date. There is nothing worse than a flash saying 'new' against an article that was put on the site three months ago. Keeping the site up to date takes time, and there is no point embarking on a site unless you have budgeted the time for updating regularly.

- **Can we guarantee to respond to interest our site generates?** If you put your e-mail address on your Web site, or include a form where people can respond, they will expect you to do something with the messages they send – and they will expect a quicker response than by post. You must make sure that it is part of someone's job to check regularly and handle responses promptly.

- **How will people find our site?** You have to put just as much effort into publicising a Web site as you do a printed publication. Some people may stumble across it, but most will need to be led there, either by your own publicity, or by links from other sites. You will need to work hard to get these links established.

- **Are we trying to cut corners?** Just as with paper-based publishing, you can elect to do it on the cheap, but on the Web you are often competing for attention with the professionals. In most cases you will be better off using a good professional designer to set your site up, and to get both the design and the technology right.

Having looked at all these questions, you still have to solve the practical problems – such as which service provider you will use, and whether to have your own 'domain name'.

Using the Internet for research

As staff become familiar with using the Internet, and particularly the Web, they may start to ask for access from work. For certain types of worker this is well worth considering, but the normal decision-making process should be applied: what are we trying to achieve, what are the options, and what are the costs, benefits and risks?

Providing access is rarely a problem. E-mail accounts normally give automatic Web access as well; the software is readily available; and networks can allow multiple users to have Web access at the same time.

More and more valuable material is available on the Web. As well as commercial sites, many government departments now put key information on the Web. Other voluntary organisations may have sites you can use productively, and the Web can also be a good way of linking people around the world in an issue-based community.

It is worth becoming familiar with two types of site that provide an entry-point to the mass of material on the Web.

- Search engines will trawl through all the information on the Web that they are aware of, looking for keywords. Many have a US bias, and some have become discredited because their results are weighted in favour of those sites which have paid for a place higher up the list.
- 'Portals' are sites which guide you to other sites that are related to specific topics, possibly with an assessment of the content. As well as the consumer-oriented portals, many specialist organisations are now setting up portals with links to other sites in their field. These take a lot of the work out of finding information, and are a good example of the principle of 'using the experts'.

Before enabling access to the Web, you do need to satisfy yourself on a number of concerns.

- If you allow Web access, should it be for all staff, or just those who can demonstrate a need? If you think only the latter, then think also what messages you are sending about trust or about belief in staff capacity to contribute.
- Will staff time be productively spent? Is the Web really the best place to get the information needed? (Often the answer is, indeed, yes.)
- Are you able to ensure that you provide suitable training to enable your staff to use the Web effectively for serious research, not just idle browsing?
- Will your 'bandwidth' be sufficient? (In other words, do you have fast enough access?) A simple modem which is adequate for a considerable number of e-mail users may well buckle under the strain of even a few Web users who need to be on-line for longer and to transfer larger amounts of data. The next step up in speed is an ISDN line, with faster speeds yet available from ADSL or cable access.
- Do you have policies in place to spell out the kind of uses of the Web you regard as unacceptable? While pornographic and extreme sites are obviously out, what about private use – news, sport, weather, holiday bookings and the like?

Other computer-based systems

Software is available for handling specific tasks related to information management, such as accounting systems, personnel systems and contact managers. Each of these fulfils a well-defined role, and the process of deciding whether to invest in one, and if so in which, has been described above in this chapter.

Some of the systems that specifically promote information-sharing and collaborative working are worth describing here in a bit more detail. These include:

- mailing lists and other extensions of e-mail;
- systems to allow people at different computers to work on the same documents, either consecutively or at the same time;
- 'groupware';
- video conferencing.

Once people have e-mail they can subscribe to **mailing lists** where they ask to be sent information on a specific topic. This can be a very cheap way to distribute material to a defined group of people, and the technology is neither expensive nor complex.

The next step up is to allow people to make their own contributions to on-going **discussions**. Typically, the discussion is laid out in 'threads', with each main topic being followed by replies, then replies to the replies, and so on. Subscribers can choose to see just the main topics or to expand them, at will, to show the subsequent contributions as well. Any subscriber can start off a new main topic if they wish. The best discussion groups are 'moderated', which means that contributions are first checked to ensure that they are relevant to the discussion and comply with any rules of the group.

Access to discussion groups can often be made through standard e-mail software. The software required to set up and run the group is little more complex than a mailing-list server.

Sharing documents can be as simple as e-mailing them to different people, or having access to a common directory on a network. For many organisations this may be sufficient. Most word-processors, including Microsoft Word, allow quite sophisticated control over 'ownership' of documents and the power to use or modify them, as well as keeping track of changes made by different users.

Networks may also allow users to share **diaries** – including being able to make provisional appointments in each others' diaries – and **address books**.

More technically complex are systems where two or more people working on different computers can each see the same document at the same time, along with changes as people make them. This allows people to work collaboratively over a distance.

Systems which combine a number of these technologies – and more – are often described as '**groupware**'. The best-known of these is probably Lotus Notes. For those who can afford a five- or six-figure sum, this provides a complete environment where aspects of the way the organisation works can be built into the system. A database can hold key data, and documents can be linked to specific records in the database. 'Workflow' can be built into documents, so that once one person has carried out a task the document is automatically sent to the next person who has to act on it. All the elements of e-mail, discussions, diaries, common address books and shared data are included. For an organisation which is very clear about what it is trying to achieve, this is a very powerful set of tools, but at a significant cost.

Technology changes so fast that it is unwise in a book to devote much time to specific developments. It is clear, however, that information management and 'knowledge management' are areas where a lot is happening.

The authors are extremely sceptical about computer systems that are claimed to incorporate so much knowledge and experience that decision making becomes easy or even automatic.

However, any products that can be used to promote collaborative work and information sharing are worth considering, whether a simple intranet or a more elaborate product. Such products can support everyone working on a particular project, by pulling together in one place relevant documents, e-mail links to everyone working on the project, links to the project plan, links to background information and research on the subject. Where people are working on a number of projects at the same time, perhaps in different teams with volunteers, part time staff or job shares, such shared information space can be a valuable aid to productivity. Of course, the question remains whether such software will justify its often considerable price.

chapter ⑫

LOOKING AHEAD

What is the 'information society'?

We are living in an information society. This means that information, rather than labour or machinery, has come to be seen as the key resource – the one which makes the difference between profit and loss, success or failure. The theory is that, in a global economy, two competing companies will have similar access to capital and labour. It is how they create and use information – in market research, in internal organisation and in relation to customers – that will determine which company is more successful.

This is linked to the explosion of new possibilities of what can be done with information created by new technologies. The result is the change we see all around us. Organisations, industries and governments identify new information flows which they believe will make them more effective and they re-organise accordingly.

This change has a huge impact on the social domain, the one most occupied by the voluntary sector. The impact is partly indirect, through the restructuring of the economy and of employment, and in the new habits and skills people acquire as they adapt to new circumstances. It is also direct as government, quangos and the voluntary sector itself think how to implement new understandings and new technologies in their area of work.

Of course, and as always, what happens in the social domain is not just an extension of market behaviour but also a matter of political choice. One can have all the information one could ever need about a problem without the funds to do anything about it. It could be said that a traditional role of the voluntary sector is precisely that of collecting information about an issue, and then either lobbying for funds or raising them directly in order to do something about it. However, it would be a mistake for voluntary-sector organisations to take refuge in the familiar. The society and the communities in which they operate are also being re-organised. They can either try to shape that change or be its victims.

'The report ... indicates that 75% of all business communications are now undertaken through electronic media ... Yet senior management has been slow to appreciate the revolutionary consequences for corporate culture, management structure and working relationships.'
Review of *Nil by Mouth*, from Investors in People UK and Arthur Andersen, in *Flexible Working*, November 1998.

Strategic threats and opportunities

The government has set a target for the UK to become the most 'on-line' large, wealthy country (the USA, France and Canada have similar ambitions). Within the next ten years the combined forces of deliberate government policy, electronic commerce and digital television will mean that the large majority (perhaps as much as 95%) of the population will be receiving information, goods and services on-line – either via computers or via televisions.

No one knows exactly how such a rapid and extensive change will come about, or what sort of society will exist once it has. Some of the possible scenarios are potentially horrific for the voluntary sector.

- The information highway may be dominated by a small number of profit-driven cartels, each combining some mix of entertainment, home-shopping, financial services, and whatever public information and services the government makes available in negotiation with its private-sector 'partners'. Community- and voluntary-sector information may be permitted only in a sanitised form, or it may be supplied from 'professional' or commercial sources.
- Government agencies may become so successful in interactive service delivery and information provision that the role of the voluntary sector as an intermediary becomes redundant.
- Alternatively, if interaction between the public service and the citizen takes place in people's homes, it may become harder for voluntary-sector organisations to find out what is going on or to reach people and help them.
- The state may have so much influence on the design of the information systems used that, although there may appear to be room for interaction and consultation, these are in fact constrained by the way the system is set up – a bit like those multiple-choice questionnaires which never actually give you the choice you want.
- New layers of deprivation may be created among those unable to participate in the electronic nirvana.

However, there are also real opportunities for shaping what happens. Even as most large public organisations begin to have their own 'information-society' strategy, there is no overall masterplan. You don't need anyone's permission to get involved. Voluntary- and community-sector organisations can and are influencing the process either by creating partnerships with other sectors or simply by doing things themselves. There are a number of positive factors to help them in this process.

- Many policy-makers actually want all this to work. They recognise that, like any other computer-based activity, the 'information society' is only likely to work if the users are involved in its creation. They prefer an economic model where millions are using the technology to generate new ideas and new information content, rather than one of couch-based consumers.

- Many government agencies at all levels recognise that anything they do by themselves is less likely to be effective than work they do in collaboration with others. This is partly the agenda of 'joined-up government' but there is some openness to further 'joining up' with the community and voluntary sectors. This opens the possibility of information from these sources becoming far more available to both public-service managers and the public.

- There are limitless ways in which new technologies can be used to improve the internal functioning of voluntary-sector organisations, the exchange of information between them and their interaction with their stakeholders. Barriers to participation created by time, mobility, sight or sound may be reduced. There is huge potential to use multimedia – sound, picture, video – to lessen the alienation created by endless words and jargon.

Local strategies

This, you may say, is all very well but what can a small voluntary-sector organisation do? Most such organisations already feel over-worked and under-resourced. Thinking beyond the expiry date of the current project funding is never easy, even in a context of local processes which are well understood, let alone those of seismic global change. In addition, the voluntary sector's relationship with computers is just as ambiguous as everyone else's. It uses them a lot – in South Yorkshire, for example, a higher percentage of community- and voluntary-sector organisations use computers than do small businesses. But that doesn't mean it is easy to make things work as they are supposed to, to get on-line when the administrator is using the computer to complete last year's accounts, or to pay the phone bill for extensive on-line work.

We are not arguing that this information revolution is wonderful. We are simply stating that it exists. Organisations which want to survive, let alone prosper, will have to adapt to what is happening and to help the people with whom they work adapt too. This does not usually require sudden or drastic change. There are a number of steps organisations can and should be taking to ensure that they are not cast adrift.

- Keep an eye on what others – the government, quangos and other voluntary-sector organisations – are doing on 'information-society' issues in your area of work. Even if you don't have the time to attend endless meetings, look out for news items, talk to people, attend the occasional briefing or conference.
- Remember that it is the information which has value, not the technology (unless you are a major shareholder in Microsoft!). Try to use the techniques described in this book to manage your own information well. An organisation which uses its own information efficiently, and which has good-quality information on its specialist area ready to give others, in a form they can use, will fare better in our information society than an organisation confused by numerous but badly set-up computers.
- Explore ways in which information and communication technologies could be used imaginatively in your specialist area of work. Don't worry about it at your desk. Think about who else could be involved – 'clients', friends, family, local schools, MA students from your local university – to brainstorm new ideas.
- Work with 'clients' to see if and how they are coming to use the tools of the information age. Explore ways of learning together. Helping each other enter this new world is likely to do far more for your long-term relationship than coming to it via different brands of on-line shopping.

Example 24 Local technology

Community arts, local history and archive projects are springing up all over the country. One of the earliest to use new computer technologies – Artimedia in Batley, West Yorkshire – used e-mail to link schoolchildren with pensioners to discuss local history. Such linkages, properly managed, can create opportunities for both sets of participants which go far beyond the immediate objectives of exploring local history.

Some organisations assume that 'their' people aren't going to be interested in these newfangled ideas. We have heard 30-year old managers say this, while in the background 90-year-olds are e-mailing their great grandchildren in Australia. Nearly everyone can and will use some form of interactive information device.

Finally, there is no reason for individual organisations to think through all this by themselves. Voluntary-sector organisations must resist the temptation to see each other as competitors for funds, rather than organisations with similar values, which have many common interests.

When voluntary-sector organisations do work together they have an attitude to getting things done and a flexibility which can leave compartmentalised bureaucracies standing. The information society is one area which is begging for co-operation within the voluntary and community sector. It is also an area in which this sector can take a lead – having more knowledge of both the potential and the pitfalls of electronic communication than many of the individuals and organisations who are, on paper, 'in charge' of developments. Fortunately, there is considerable progress in this area, often encouraged by the formation of new organisations and partnerships which specialise in information.

Leading-edge developments

At community level, community information projects, community training enterprises and electronic village halls are springing up, trying to raise local awareness of the potential of the new technologies. Such projects can also explore the potential of bringing together information at a local level as a resource for local people and organisations. Such locally collected information resources can challenge the perspectives of information previously collected through more bureaucratic approaches by public-sector organisations.

At city or county level, various partnerships exist to bring a strategic approach to the development of an information society in their geographic area. Such partnerships vary in their openness, equality and understanding of information and how it flows. All claim to be interested in a 'socially inclusive' information society. Many require, for funding (and especially European funding) purposes, the active involvement of voluntary and community organisations. These requirements offer scope for significant input from the voluntary and community sectors even in cases where the sincerity of some of the partners is in doubt.

At national and European levels, organisations such as UK Communities On-Line and the European Association of Community Networks exist and are growing. Membership-based organisations, they aim to share experiences, develop new ideas and ensure that the leading-edge experience of many of their local, community-based members is acknowledged and learned from in the development of public policy.

The slogan of one of the founder members of the European Association of Community Networks, the Milan Civic Network, is 'The network is you', 'you' meaning the Network members. Although all the usual prejudices and disparities of wealth and power remain, the fact is that existing relationships are being challenged by new flows of information. There is no certainty about the outcome of these changes, but there are opportunities for the voluntary and community sector both to improve its own practice and to influence wider changes. In the future, it must be said – 'the information society is us'.

FURTHER INFORMATION

Publications

Clear Your Desk: the definitive guide to mastering your paper workload for ever, Declan Treacy, Arrow Business Books, 1998

A clear and easy-to-read guide to reducing your own paperwork. Covers many of the same ideas as Chapter 5, but in more detail and with more specific examples.

Data Protection for Voluntary Organisations, Paul Ticher, available from Directory of Social Change, 2000

The only comprehensive publication to look at this important topic specifically from a voluntary-sector perspective.

Education & Training for Information Work in the Voluntary Sector (British Library Research & Information Report 156), Rebecca Linley, Sally Gibbs, Dave Muddiman, Sue Tuffin and Jackie Urwin, 1999

A look at what information workers in the voluntary sector actually do, and a somewhat contentious look at their training needs.

Get Organised: Save time and improve your productivity by clearing the clutter, Odette Pollar, Kogan Page, 1992

One of several books in this resource section that gives practical steps towards reducing your own paperwork, covering the type of material in Chapter 5.

Get Yourself Organised, Mike Levy, David Grant Publishing, 1997

Starts with a short section on clearing your desk, then covers prioritising, delegation, procrastination, meetings and computers.

The Informability Manual: Making Information More Accessible in the Light of the Disability Discrimination Act, Wendy Gregory, The Stationery Office, 1996

An invaluable comprehensive guide, looking first at the needs of different types of audience, then at how to approach information in different media.

The Information Age: Economy, Society and Culture: Volume 1, The Rise of the Network Society; Volume 2, The Power of Identity; and Volume 3, End of the Millennium, Manuel Castells, Blackwells, 1996-98

Not a short read, and the author is threatened with guru status, but these books mix a mass of evidence with strong arguments about the causes of global change and the role of information within it. For those without a pleasant week (fortnight?) of leisure to enjoy these books at their best, the main argument is very succinctly summarised in a paper prepared for the UNRISD Conference on Information Technologies and Social Development, in Geneva, which is available at: http://www.unrisd.org/infotech/conferen/castelp1.htm

Information Management for Development Organisations, Mike Powell, Oxfam, 1999

A book for managers in international development organisations helping them to think through the awareness and skills they need to manage information in a fast-changing area of work. Its value for readers of this book may lie in the greater detail and the examples it offers of the tools mentioned in Chapter 9 of this book.

Information Management in the Voluntary Sector, Diana Grimwood-Jones and Sylvia Simmons (eds), ASLIB, 1998

A comprehensive selection of academic papers looking at how the voluntary sector actually manages its information, as well as giving advice and suggestions based on examples of good practice.

Job Descriptions for the Information Profession, Mary Casteleyn, ASLIB, 1996

A short book, part of the ASLIB Know How Series, with examples of job descriptions for librarians and other information workers, plus guidance on how to prepare your own job descriptions.

Managing IT, Paul Ticher with Martin Jones, London Advice Services Alliance, 1998

Expands on much of the material included in Chapter 11 here, and includes useful checklists for assessing how well you are doing.

The Plain English Guide, Martin Cutts, Oxford University Press, 1996

An excellent guide to writing clear, easily understandable English.

The Voluntary Sector Legal Handbook, Sandy Adirondack and James Sinclair Taylor, available from Directory of Social Change, 1996

The essential reference on every legal topic for all voluntary-sector managers.

Thirty Minutes to Manage Information Overload, John Caunt, Kogan Page, 1999

A rapid sweep through a number of personal information overload issues, with practical suggestions for action.

Web sites

In general, printing the addresses of Web sites in books is asking for trouble as many sites have a transient life. Here are a few which should be longer-lasting and which might repay attention.

www.ncvo-vol.org.uk/main/gateway/index.html This page, maintained by NCVO, functions as an on-line index to the voluntary sector. You can use it to explore the work of many organisations, or if you have a Web site which is not listed on it, you can ask to be added to it.

www.communities.org.uk This is the page of UK Communities On-Line, a not-for-profit organisation which is in the process of becoming a membership organisation owned by the growing number of community-based information projects. From its pages you can find links to virtually every such project in the UK, to European Union networks, and to various expert sites relating to the same subject.

www.womenconnect.org.uk is the web site of a project pioneering the use of internet technology by a range of women's organisations. The link to their November 1999 conference provides further food for thought on issues of gender in the information society.

www.w3.organisation/WAI

www.austin.ibm.com/sns/

goodpractices.com/

www.cast.org/bobby

These are all sites which give advice and information to people specifying the design for or actually designing Web pages to ensure maximum levels of accessibility, while the National Library for the Blind (www.nlbuk.org) is a prize-winning example of site design.

www.thebrain.com and *www.mindmanager.com/* are two sites offering tools to assist you in portraying your information systems.

Organisations

London Advice Services Alliance
Universal House
88–94 Wentworth Street
London
E1 7SA
020 7377 1226 (for IT enquiries)
020 7377 2748 (for publications and general enquiries)
e-mail: info@lasa.org.uk
One of the longest-established voluntary-sector support units for information, advice and IT-related topics. Offers invaluable training and publications, including a series of guides and training courses on managing IT, and **Computanews***, a bi-monthly non-technical IT newsletter for the voluntary sector.*

Royal National Institute for the Blind (RNIB)
224 Great Portland Street, London W1N 6AA
020 7388 1266
Produce useful guidance on preparing information so that it is accessible to visually-impaired people.

VOLSIF (the Voluntary Sector Information Forum)
An informal group of information workers in the voluntary sector which meets several times a year in London and maintains an e-mail contact list.
Contact Briony Milligan at NCVO for details.
020 7520 2508 (direct line)
briony.milligan@ncvo-vol.org.uk